Author's note

Learning grammar is a simple process when taken step by step. Experience has shown that children and indeed students of all ages delight in its logical, systematic order. Each word in a sentence plays its own part, forming a complete pattern in which everything fits; nothing can be left over. An exercise in grammar is an exercise in logic and, as such, plays a vital part in the development of logical thought.

I have regularly shared the delight of students whose faces light up with understanding and the stimulation of successful reasoning. I wish you all that same joy of discovery and satisfaction gained from this knowledge of language to which I believe everyone has a right.

Grammar Made Easy

Barbara Dykes

Hale & Iremonger

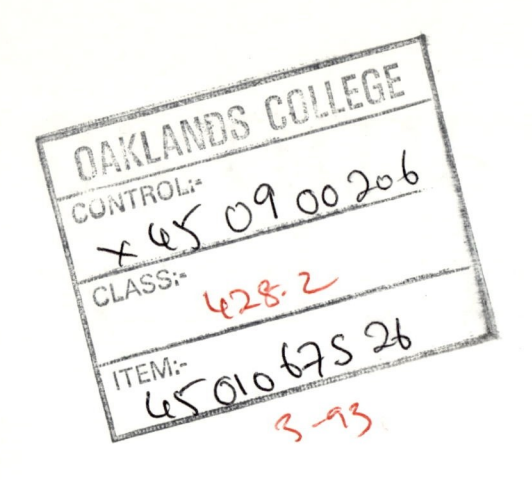

© 1992 by Barbara Dykes

This book is copyright. Apart from any fair dealing for the purposes of study, research, criticism, review, or as otherwise permitted under the Copyright Act, no part may be reproduced by any process without written permission. Inquiries should be made to the publisher.

Typeset, printed & bound by
Southwood Press Pty Limited
80–92 Chapel Street, Marrickville, NSW

For the publisher
Hale & Iremonger Pty Limited
GPO Box 2552, Sydney, NSW

National Library of Australia Cataloguing-in-publication entry

Dykes, Barbara, 1933-
    Grammar made easy.

    Includes index.
    ISBN 0 86806 409 2.

    1. English language — Grammar — 1950-   2. English language
    — Grammar — 1950-   — Problems, exercises, etc. I. Title.

428.2

Contents

Authors' note   *1*
Introduction   *7*

Part One   The parts of speech
1. Nouns   *11*
2. Pronouns   *14*
3. Verbs   *20*
4. Adjectives   *31*
5. Adverbs   *36*
6. Prepositions   *38*
7. Articles, conjunctions, and interjections   *40*
8. Parsing   *42*
9. Sentences   *45*
    Exercises   *50*

Part Two   Punctuation
10. Capital letters   *63*
11. The full stop   *65*
12. The comma   *67*
13. The question mark   *69*
14. The exclamation mark   *70*
15. Inverted commas   *72*
16. The apostrophe   *74*
17. The semicolon   *77*

Grammar Made Easy

    18   The colon   *79*
    19   Parentheses and dashes   *80*
           Exercises   *82*

Part Three   **More about verbs**
    20   Verbs: transitive and intransitive   *89*
    21   Voice: active and passive   *91*
    22   Perfect tenses   *92*
    23   Emphatic tenses   *96*
    24   Participles as verbs and adjectives   *98*
    25   Participles as nouns (gerunds)   *100*
    26   Mood   *102*
           Exercises   *104*

Part Four   **Sentences: more about clauses and phrases**
    27   Case   *111*
    28   Phrases   *116*
    29   Clauses   *119*
    30   Sentence analysis   *130*
           Exercises   *133*

Part Five   **Get it right**
    31   Some common mistakes explained   *141*
    32   Know the difference!   *147*
           Exercises   *163*

Part Six   **Answers to exercises**
           Part One   *175*
           Part Two   *180*
           Part Three   *181*
           Part Four   *183*
           Part Five   *184*

Index   *187*

Introduction

> *A knowledge of grammatical terminology provides us with a language in which we can discuss language*
> T. P. Hackett

Grammar is about knowing how to put words together correctly to make sense. It is about knowing the part that each word plays in a sentence so that we can both understand it in reading and use it correctly in writing. It is about having terms for each word according to its function so that we can refer to it and discuss it. With this knowledge we learn to develop greater awareness of meaningful language and skill in using it competently.

How can explanations about language be given to a student who has been deprived of training in elementary grammar?

For example, without knowing the terms, let alone the function of parts of speech, imagine trying to understand this rule: The distinction between 'dependant' and 'dependent' is that the noun ends in 'ant', the adjective in 'ent'.

Earlier in the century grammar books were complicated, loaded with inessential and unnecessary terms, of value chiefly to linguists. They needed revision; but by eliminating grammar from the curriculum, countless young people have been deprived of one of the basic elements of scholarship — an understanding of the function of words.

Not only is a sound knowledge of the workings of our language part of our rightful cultural heritage, it is also important when learning foreign languages. Moreover, the study of grammar provides valuable training and exercise in logical thinking and is of paramount importance for mental development.

The value of grammatical training was never better explained than it was by W. B. Yeats. When asked at the end of his career how he always succeeded in making his meaning clear even on the most obscure subjects, he declared,

> 'The answer is simple. I was drilled in grammar and syntax at school.'

Part One

The parts of speech

1. Nouns
2. Pronouns
3. Verbs
4. Adjectives
5. Adverbs
6. Prepositions
7. Articles, conjunctions, and interjections
8. Parsing
9. Kinds of sentences

common noun
boy
dog
bone

proper noun
Australia
Tasmania

collective noun
audience
group

abstract noun
joy, pleasure
happiness

1
Nouns

Nouns are the names of things. Everything that exists, every person, place or thing has a name. Even those things we cannot see, but exist in our minds, have a name — eg truth.

THE FOUR KINDS OF NOUNS

Common nouns (the names of things): applies to *any* one of a class of things.

nail	horse	girl
ant	water	chair
car	pencil	tweezers

Proper nouns (special names of people, places, etc.): applies to a *particular* one in a class of people or things.

Australia	Jenny	Don
Canberra	April	Santa Clause
Sunday	Africa	Woolworths

Collective nouns (names for groups of things)

team	herd	class
band	swarm	collection
litter	convoy	jury

Abstract nouns (names of things we cannot see but which exist in our minds)

love	joy	greed
happiness	thought	worry
memories	concentration	foolishness

SINGULAR AND PLURAL (NUMBER)

A noun can be the name for one thing,
        eg screwdriver (singular),
or for more than one thing
        eg screwdrivers (plural).

Singular	*Plural*
torch	torches
leg	legs
sandwich	sandwiches
man	men
lorry	lorries
tortoise	tortoises
mouse	mice

MASCULINE, FEMININE, OR NEUTER (GENDER)

Nouns can also be male or female. If they are neither, we call them neuter.

Masculine	*Feminine*
boy	girl
man	woman
father	mother
king	queen
duke	duchess
actor	actress
drake	duck
fox	vixen
bull	cow
ram	ewe

Nouns

Neuter

person	piano
bicycle	bible
blister	hooter
potato	zip
pork	market

POSSESSION

If a noun owns something we call it **possessive**.

Jack's belt	mother's ring
baby's plate	teacher's ruler
the school's headmaster	Paddy's market

If the noun which possesses something is plural, we put an apostrophe after its s.

the dogs' bones
the boys' parents
the cars' windows
the teachers' meeting
the Scouts' adventure

For more about using apostrophes, see pp. 74-6.

John's
|
proper noun
singular
masculine
possessive

sons
|
common noun
plural
masculine

2
Pronouns

Pronouns are the words that we can use *in place of nouns,* so that we can avoid repetition or clumsiness.

Instead of:
> Fiona beat the eggs till the eggs were light and fluffy.

We can say:
> Fiona beat the eggs till **they** were light and fluffy.

Instead of:
> Malcolm sounds like a frog when Malcolm sings.

We can say:
> Malcolm sounds like a frog when **he** sings.

PERSONAL PRONOUNS

Personal pronouns that do the work of the *subject:*

	Singular	Plural
1st Person	I	we
(the person speaking)		
2nd Person	you	you
(the person spoken to)	*thou/thee	*ye
3rd Person	he/she/it	they
(the person being spoken about)		

Examples:
> **She** dropped the ice-cream.
> **It** fell off a truck.
> **They** climbed onto the fence.
> **We** sang songs till midnight.

Personal pronouns that do the work of the *object:*

	Singular	Plural
1st Person (the person speaking)	me	us
2nd Person (the person spoken to)	you	you
	*thee	*ye
3rd Person (the person spoken about)	him/her/it	them

Examples:
> The ball hit **me**.
> Jenny cleaned **it**.
> The teacher likes **you**.
> The bus left **them** behind.
> Will the dog hurt **us**?

POSSESSIVE PRONOUNS

These stand in place of a noun which is owned by someone/some people.

	Singular	Plural
1st Person (the person speaking)	mine	ours
2nd Person (the person spoken to)	yours *thine	yours
3rd Person (the person spoken about)	his/her/its	their

---
* used in the Bible, poetry, old writing.

Examples:
> She lent me **hers**.
> The dinner is **mine**.
> We like **yours**, I hope you like **ours**.

Note
My, your, their, his, etc. are adjectives because they qualify (describe) a noun but do not replace it. You cannot say 'That is my'. These words are sometimes called possessive adjectives.

> This is **my** soup.
> Where is **your** calculator?
> Did Lucy bring **her** dog?
> Put the game back into **its** box.

Remember that, in this case, its has no apostrophe. (It's can only mean it is.)

OTHER KINDS OF PRONOUNS

The simple rule is that a word is a pronoun if it is standing in the place of a noun.

There are different names for pronouns according to the job they do in the sentence. It is not necessary to learn the different kinds at this stage but the names help us to understand why certain words are pronouns.

RELATIVE PRONOUNS

| who | whom |
| which | that |

They are called relative because they relate (or are linked to) a noun which they stand for.

> I met a crooked man **who** had a crooked smile.
> You can have the cake **which** is in the oven.
> George has some toffee **that** is very sticky.
> He was the leader **whom** you chose.

REFLEXIVE PRONOUNS (or emphatic pronouns)

Singular	Plural
myself	ourselves
yourself	yourselves
himself/herself/itself	themselves

These are called reflexive pronouns because they 'turn back' to the person already mentioned to give emphasis:

> I did it **myself**.
> You can do it **yourselves**.
> The cat hurt **itself**
> They caught the thief **themselves**.

DEMONSTRATIVE PRONOUNS

Singular	Plural
this	that
these	those

They are called demonstrative because they demonstrate or point out which one (ones) is being talked about.

> **This** is mine.
> **That** is yours.
> David gave me **those**.
> **These** are his.

The demonstrative pronoun stands for 'this/that one', the noun that is not mentioned.

Remember: if the noun is mentioned the words identifying which particular noun are called adjectives.

This is bad	**This** apple is bad
Pronoun	*Adjective*

INTERROGATIVE PRONOUNS

who	which
whom	whose
what	

These are the pronouns used for asking questions.

> **Who** are you?

Which way did he go?
Whom did you see?
Whose are these?
What is your name?

Whom is used to stand for a person or people who are the **object** of the sentence.

Whom did the police catch?
Object

Douglas gave (to) **whom** the cherries?
Indirect object *Object*

INDEFINITE PRONOUNS

one, everyone   anything
anybody, anyone   nothing
nobody, no-one   something
somebody, someone   everything

These pronouns do not refer to a particular person or thing.

Everybody loves **someone.**
I am bored if I have **nothing** to do.
Everyone enjoyed Expo.

DISTRIBUTIVE PRONOUNS

each   either   neither

These pronouns refer to one only. Each refers to one or two or more. Either and neither refer to one of two only.

Each of us has a book.
Either of you may go.
Neither of them wears glasses.

It is important to note that these pronouns are in the singular because they refer to one only. Therefore the verb that follows must be in the singular also.

Each   **has**   a lunch box.
pronoun   *verb*
 singular

Pronouns

Either is satisfactory.
*pronoun verb
  singular*

Neither comes on Saturdays.
*pronoun verb
  singular*

Remember: Some words are pronouns when they stand on their own, but are adjectives when they accompany the noun they qualify. See p. 31.

Examples:

These are wearing out.
demonstrative pronoun

These shoes are wearing out.
demonstrative adjective noun

This is **his**.
*demonstrative   possessive
pronoun   pronoun*

This bag is **his**.
*possessive noun   possessive
adjective   pronoun*

This is **his bag**.
*demonstrative   possessive noun
pronoun   adjective*

3
Verbs

Verbs are doing, being or having words.

INFINITE AND FINITE VERBS

Infinitives do not have a subject and do not show a sense of time. Sometimes we put to in front of the verb when we refer to the infinitive.

    to skate   to go
    to spend   to ride
    to leave   to read
    to complete   to make
    to illustrate   to magnify

Finite verbs have a subject and do include a sense of time. This is called *tense*.

TENSE

Present tense — something is happening now

    Monica writes.
    Jack is welding.
    We are riding our bikes.
    My sister is making ice cream.
    The kettle is boiling.

They have bad manners.
Who is shouting?
Than man has a bad leg.

Past tense — something has happened already
Mark fell off is bike.
The little girl was crying.
He wrote a letter.
Grandad called the doctor.
Stephen won the race.
My hat blew off.
The frogs were jumping away.

Future tense — something has not yet happened
We shall go to Queensland.
Christmas will come soon.
You will have presents.
Mother will take us to the Pantomime.
Jenny will be dancing at the concert.
When will you leave?
Who will make the tea?

Now you see that you can make a complete sentence with a noun and a verb.

The wind   is blowing.
verb   *verb*

This doll   talks.
noun   *verb*

Mother   will come.
noun   *verb*

The girls   are crying.
noun   *verb*

SUBJECTS

Finite verbs have a subject. The subject of a sentence is the person or thing that the sentence is about.

Sally has an ice cream.

Lisa is tall.
Daddy has a car.
Grandad fought at Gallipoli.
It never rains on Sundays.
Carrots are good for you.

The subject does not always come at the beginning of the sentence.

On Tuesdays **we** go to the Boys' Brigade.
Before going home **Ted** phoned the Pizza Hut.
Due to a hailstorm **the farmer** has lost all his crops.

A subject can be more than one word.

Three blind mice ran after the farmer's wife.
Flying aeroplanes is my favourite hobby.
Molly and I are going to have a party.

The verb must agree with its subject in person and number.

I	am late.	1st person singular
You	are late too.	2nd person singular
She	is always early.	3rd person singular
I	bring my lunch to school.	1st person singular
He	brings his lunch to school.	3rd person singular
He	has a good dictionary	3rd person singular
They	have a good dictionary	3rd person plural
I	am sorry.	1st person singular
We	are sorry.	1st person plural

OBJECTS

The object is the person or thing which 'suffers' the action of the verb.

DIRECT OBJECT

If you can ask 'what?' after the verb, the *answer* is the object.

> Mary made the bed.
> *Mary made what?*
> *Answer:* the bed
> *Therefore 'the bed' is the object.*

> The scouts lit their campfire.
>   *object*

> The dog chased the cat.
>   *object*

INDIRECT OBJECT

This is a noun or pronoun. It is the person or thing which is affected by the action of the verb.

Mary	threw	(to)	Jason	the ball
subject	*verb*		*Indirect object*	*object*

If you ask 'what?' after the verb, you get a direct object.

> *Thus:* Mary threw what?   *Answer:* the ball

Therefore the ball is the object.

But: To whom or for whom was the action done?

Answer: Jason
> (Mary threw the ball *to* Jason.)

Therefore Jason is the Indirect Object.

More examples:

Please	pass	(to) me	the jam
		Indirect Object	*Object*

We left	(to) the birds	the remains	of our picnic
	Indirect Object	*Object*	

Note: Test your indirect object by putting to or for in front of it. Does the sentence still make sense?

We left (for) the birds the remains of our picnic.

Jessica gave	the dog	a bath.
	Indirect Object	Object

PERSON

A book is written in the *First Person* when the storyteller is the subject of the story.

> I opened my eyes when the sun shone onto my pillow. Suddenly I was very excited. It was going to be a special day because it was my Birthday.

A book is written in the *Third Person* when the storyteller tells the story with someone else as the subject.

> Becky came outside with a torch in her hand. She called Woody but he did not come, so she closed the door and ran into the park to look for him.

PARTICIPLES

Participles are the parts of verbs which need a helper, called an auxiliary verb, in order to form a complete tense. There are two kinds of participle — present and past.

PRESENT PARTICIPLE

This is formed by adding ing to the verb root

Verb root	Present Participle
sing	singing
fly	flying
enchant	enchanting

The helper or auxiliary is added to the participle to form a complete tense.

> The bird is singing.
> *helper + present participle*
> *present continuous sense*

> They are flying.
> *helper + present participle*
> *present continuous tense*

PAST PARTICIPLE

This is the part of the verb which is added to a helper, or auxiliary, to form a past tense.

The verbs which end in 'ed' in the past tense have the same past participle. They are known as *regular* or *weak* verbs. See pp. 26-7.

verb	*past tense*	*past participle*
walk	walked	walked
bake	baked	baked
load	loaded	loaded
confiscate	confiscated	confiscated

Some verbs which form the past tense in another way have a different past participle. These are called *irregular* or *strong* verbs. See pp. 26-7.

verb	*past tense*	*past participle*
ride	rode	ridden
know	knew	known
ring	rang	rung
take	took	taken
drive	drove	driven
wear	wore	worn

If it sounds correct when you say 'I have' before it, then it should be the Past Participle: I have ridden.

HELPER OR AUXILIARY VERBS

The helper or auxiliary is added to the participle to form a past tense.

The verb **to have** helps to form a verb in the Active Voice:

    They   have   gone.
                  helper   *past participle*

    Lesley   has   painted   the gate.
              helper *past participle*

The verb **to be** helps to form a verb in the Passive Voice:

    Debbie   was   bitten.
              helper *past participle*

    We   were   soaked
         helper *past participle*

For more on participles, see pp. 98-101.

REGULAR AND IRREGULAR VERBS

REGULAR VERBS

These are also called *weak* verbs. All verbs whose past tense ends in **d** or **t** are regular or weak verbs.

Present	*Past*	
paint	painted	*ed* is added to
whip	whipped	form the past
complain	complained	tense.
live	lived	*d* is added to a
note	noted	word which
tease	teased	already ends in *e*.

Present	Past	
sell	sold	The past tense ends
smell	smelt	with a *d* or *t* which
buy	bought	is not there in the
weep	wept	present tense.
hurt	hurt	The past tense is
spread	spread	the same as the
put	put	present tense.

IRREGULAR VERBS

These are also called *strong* verbs. Irregular or strong verbs are all those which form the past tense by changing the inside vowel (not shortening it) and do not add a final d or t.

Present	Past	
drink	drank	inside vowel changes
dig	dug	in the past tense.
stand	stood*	

*d is already there in the present tense.

Present	Past	Past Participle	
draw	drew	drawn	the past participle
shake	shook	shaken	is formed by adding
swear	swore	sworn	*n* or *en*

STRONG — WEAK VERBS

Some strong verbs have become weak because people have treated them as weak verbs. In many cases both forms remain in use.

Present	Past	Past Participle	Weak Form
rot	rotted	rotten	rotted
prove	proved	proven	proved
shave	shaved	shaven	shaved
shear	sheared	shorn	sheared

SIMPLE OR CONTINUOUS TENSES

SIMPLE

In Simple tenses, the action of the verb is seen as complete or having an end.

> Greg **chops** the wood.
> I **shall chop** the wood.
> They **have chopped** the wood.

CONTINUOUS

In continuous tenses the present participle is used with an auxiliary or helper to show that the action is not complete but is still going on.

> Greg **is chopping** the wood.
> I **shall be chopping** the wood.
> They **have been chopping** the wood.

Note: Auxiliary or helper verbs are needed with the present participle to form a finite verb.

TENSES

	Present	Past	Future
Simple	I wave	I waved	I shall wave
Continuous	I am waving	I was waving	I shall be waving
Simple	You shake	You shook	You will shake
Continuous	You are shaking	You were shaking	You will be shaking
Simple	Mum bakes	Mum baked	Mum will bake
Continuous	Mum is baking	Mum was baking	Mum will be baking
Simple	They laugh	They laughed	They will laugh
Continuous	They are laughing	They were laughing	They will be laughing

Verbs

COMPLEMENT

Even when a verb has a subject, the sense is not always complete.

That man	is	.... (is what?)
subject	*verb*	
	predicate	

You	will be	.... (will be what?)
subject	*verb*	
	predicate	

The **complement** is what we add to the predicate to **complete** the sense of the sentence. When the verb has to do with being then the **complement** must refer to the same person or thing as the **subject**:

That man	is	the mayor.
subject	*verb*	*complement*

So the complement is *not* an object and 'being' verbs cannot take an object. They have a complement (that which complements).

My dog Woody	is	a German Shepherd.
subject	*verb 'to be'*	*complement*

Elizabeth II	is	the Queen of England.
subject	*verb 'to be'*	*complement*

Note: The complement refers to the same person or thing as the subject.

The complement can be an adjective or an adjectival phrase.

These boys	are	lazy.
subject	*verb 'to be'*	*complement*

Verbs

You	will be	late.
subject	*verb 'to be'*	*complement*

He	is	sorry.
subject	*verb 'to be'*	*complement*

Other verbs which have something to do with being can take a complement too.

Remember, the complement must refer to the same person or thing as the subject.

That young man	would make	a good actor.
subject	*verb*	*complement*

This seed	will grow into	a huge tree.
subject	*verb*	*complement*

The sailors	remained	calm.
subject	*verb*	*complement*

Fred — *proper noun, third person singular, masculine gender, subject of verb 'is loading'*

is — *auxiliary verb*

loading — *present participle*

is loading — *present continuous tense*

boxes — *common noun, neuter gender, plural, object of verb 'is loading'*

onto the

truck. — *common noun, third person, neuter gender, singular, object of preposition 'onto'*

4
Adjectives

Adjectives are describing words. They tell more about people or things. The names for people and things are nouns, so we say that adjectives **qualify** nouns.

    Coloured lollipops
    Three blind mice
    The **Holy** Bible
    All things **bright** and **beautiful**

Some words are pronouns when they are on their own, but are adjectives when they accompany the noun they describe. See p. 19.

Remember: If the word takes the place of a noun, then it is a pronoun. If the noun is mentioned then these words do the work of adjectives:

    These are mine.   *But:*   These shoes are wearing out.
    pronoun   *pronoun*   *adjective noun*

    This is his.   *But:*   This bag is his.
    pronoun *pronoun*   *adjective*   *pronoun*

    Some people sing in the street.   *But:*   Some keep quiet.
    adjective noun   *pronoun*

ADJECTIVES SHOWING DEGREE

Adjectives can show degree. The quality they describe can be possessed more or less in one case than in another.

Positive	Comparative	Superlative
long	longer	longest
fine	finer	finest
heavy	heavier	heaviest
green	greener	greenest
small	smaller	smallest

Nicky has **long** finger nails.
Tracey has **longer** finger nails (than Nicky).
Sarah has the **longest** finger nails of all.

Some of the common forms are not regular.

bad	worse	worst
much	more	most
good	better	best
little	less	least

Dennis had a **bad** cold.
Dad's cold is **worse**.
I have the **worst** cold.

Some adjectives sound clumsy with the regular endings, so **more** and **most** are used with them instead.

Positive	Comparative	Superlative
beautiful	more beautiful	most beautiful
bent	more bent	most bent
reliable	more reliable	most reliable

Examples:
What a beautiful view!
Further up the hill it is **more** beautiful.
It is **most** beautiful from the top.

Adjectives

Note: In this case, **more** and **most** are adverbs limiting the adjective that they appear before.

So: When we compare only two things, the comparative should be used.

>Joanne is **slimmer** than Betty.
>He is **older** than she is.
>Which is the **lighter** of the two boxes?
>John and Andy are twins, but Andy is **stronger**.

When more than two things are compared then the superlative is used.

>This is the **tallest** tree I have ever seen.
>Bill told the **funniest** joke!
>He is the **rudest** boy in my class.

POSSESSIVE ADJECTIVES

These adjectives qualify nouns by showing possession. They show something about who owns or possesses the noun.

>That is **your** toothbrush
>*possessive adjective* *noun*

>Where are **my** **paperclips?**
>*possessive adjective* *noun*

NUMERAL ADJECTIVES

Words which qualify nouns according to numbers are called **numeral adjectives**.

Cardinal Adjectives are those which tell how many:

I saw **three** ships.
numeral noun
adjective

Ten green bottles.
numeral adjective noun
adjective

Ordinal Adjectives show a thing's position in an order or series:

On the **twelfth** day of Christmas . . .
numeral noun
adjective

Indefinite Adjectives are those which do not give an exact number:

All creatures great and small.
numeral noun
adjective

Few people see the North Pole.
numeral noun
adjective

For definite and indefinite articles, see pp. 40-1.

FORMING ADJECTIVES FROM OTHER PARTS OF SPEECH

Many adjectives are formed from other parts of speech. The quality expressed in the base word can be used in different ways.

eg 1. From the verb **tire** meaning **make weary** or **grow weary**, we can form the following adjectives:
tired (weary) — Dad always comes home *tired* from work.
tiring (causing tiredness) — That was a *tiring* day.
tireless (does not tire) — He works with tireless energy.
tiresome (causing tiredness or annoying) — The heat was tiresome today.

Adjectives

2. From the noun **child** we can form these adjectives:
    childish (like a child but improper for an adult) — It is childish to suck your thumb.
    childlike (in the manner of a child) — He stared at the tropical fish in childlike wonder.
    childless (without children) — The childless couple decided to adopt an orphan.

3. From the adjective **weak** meaning lacking strength, come the adjectives:
    weakly (not strong or robust) — The weakly calf needed hourly feeds.
    weakish (tending to weakness) — He felt weakish after the cross country.

Also: weaker, weakest. See comparative and superlative, pp. 32-33.

For adjectival phrases, see p. 116.

For adjectival clauses, see pp. 120-21.

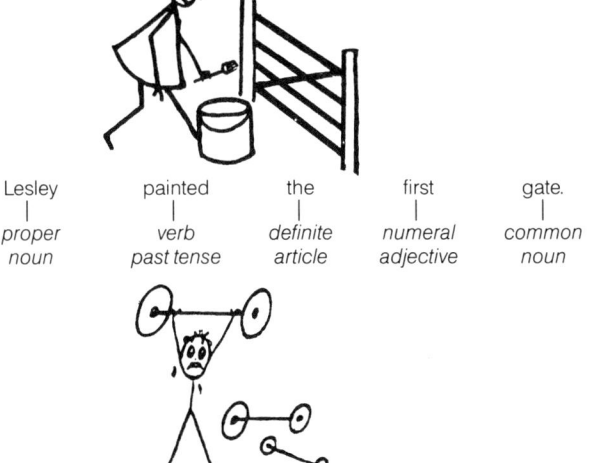

Young	Lesley	painted	the	first	gate.
adjective	proper noun	verb past tense	definite article	numeral adjective	common noun

Adjectives of degree: heavy, heavier, heaviest.

5
Adverbs

Adverbs are words which add to the meaning of verbs. They tell how, when or where something happens. We say they **modify** verbs.

        Daddy smiled **happily**.
        We rang the bell **loudly**.
        Judy swims **powerfully**.

If we add *ly* to an adjective it becomes an adverb.

        He is a **rude** boy.   He spoke **rudely**.
          adjective   *adverb*

Some adverbs tell the time or place that the verb happens.

        Let's go **now**.
        We are having a party **tomorrow**.
        Jack **always** loses his pocketbook.
        Let's drive **somewhere** for a picnic.
        We went **there** for dinner.

Adverbs can modify an adjective.

        The foot was feeling **rather** sore.
        You have been **most** helpful.
        Simon is **exceptionally** good at woodwork.

Adverbs 37

Adverbs can modify another adverb.
> She bandaged his foot **very carefully**.
> Julie is coping with her problems **rather well**.
> You are driving **too fast**.

For adverbial phrases, see pp. 116-17.

For adverbial clauses, see pp. 121-27.

She	sings	rather	sweetly.
|	|	|	|
Personal	verb	adverb	adverb
pronoun	present tense	modifying	modifying
singular		adverb	verb
feminine gender		'sweetly'	'sang'
subject of verb			
'sang'			

His	foot	was	rather	sore.
|	|	|	|	|
Possessive	common	verb	adverb	adjective
adjective	noun	past tense	modifying	describing
describing	singular		adjective	noun 'sore'
noun 'foot'	neuter gender		'sore'	

6
Prepositions

Prepositions are placed in front of nouns (or pronouns) to form a phrase. The phrase shows the relationship of one thing to another, usually according to place.

on	The bird sat **on** the branch.
through	They ran **through** the tunnel.
under	The cat crawled **under** the fence.
across	Who will come **across** the bridge?
with	She played **with** her cousins.
near	I live **near** the park.
beside	Who played **beside** the creek.
over	The town is **over** the next hill.
from	The hobo travelled **from** place to place.
up	The army climbed **up** the cliff.
in	Without waiting the children leapt **in** the pool.
among	For years she lived **among** the gorillas.

Prepositions **usually** have an object. See pp. 22-23.

Note: Often words which look like prepositions do not have an object. That is, they do not show the relationship of one thing *to another.* These are usually adverbs.

Prepositions

stand **up**
look **round**

For compound adverbs, see pp. 43-4.

Prepositions: into, above, below, etc.

7
Articles, conjunctions and interjections

ARTICLES

There are only three articles: **a**, **an**, **the**.

INDEFINITE ARTICLES: A, AN

When we use a or an we are speaking of one in numbers, but not any particular one:

> Please may I have **a** pencil?
> I found **a** sock in my pocket.

a is used before a consonant:

> **a** stick   **a** ghost
> **a** room   **a** calculator

an is used before a vowel:

> **an** ant   **an** inch
> **an** egg   **an** octopus
> **an** uncle

40

DEFINITE ARTICLE: THE

We use the when we are speaking of a particular one (singular) or ones (plural)

> Jack is driving **the** tractor.
> Please ring **the** bell.
> Stack **the** plates in **the** dishwasher.
> **The** flowers are dead.

CONJUNCTIONS

Conjunctions are joining words. They join together words or parts of a sentence.

Joining two words:

and	eggs **and** bacon
	cats **and** dogs
or	tea **or** coffee
but	cold **but** sunny

Joining two parts of a sentence:

> The alarm rang **until** the police arrived.
> We got no dinner **because** there was a power cut.
> Nero fiddled **while** Rome burnt.
> We were soaked to the skin **although** we wore our raincoats.

INTERJECTIONS

These are the words 'thrown in amongst' the other words. They have no meaning but are sounds expressing a kind of feeling.

Alas!	Ah!
Oh!	Yuk!

8
Parsing

The word *parsing* comes from a Latin word pars meaning *part*. If you parse you separate something into separate parts.

Once you have learnt the different parts of speech then parsing is easy and fun. It is a 'sorting out' process like doing a puzzle. There is a place for everything and nothing can be left over.

There are two parts in parsing:

1. Firstly, we can parse a sentence: We divide it into parts of speech.

The	early	bird	catches	the	worm.
article	*adjective*	*noun*	*verb*	*article*	*noun*

2. Secondly, we can say all that we know about each word in turn. Remember, for example, the different things we can say about a noun: kind, person, number, gender, case.

So we can parse our sentence in this way:

The: *definite article*
early: *adjective, qualifying the noun* **bird**
bird: *noun, common, 3rd person, singular, masculine or feminine, nominative case, subject of verb* **catches**
catches: *verb, transitive, present simple tense, active voice, indicative mood*
the: *definite article*
worm: *noun, common, 3rd person, singular, neuter, accusative case, object of verb* **catches**

Parsing

Captain Cook sailed slowly along the coast in his small ship *Endeavour*.

Captain Cook: *noun, proper, 3rd person, singular, masculine, nominative case, subject of verb* **sailed**
sailed: *verb, intransitive, past simple tense, active voice, indicative mood*
slowly: *adverb modifying verb* **sailed**
along: *preposition governing* **coast**
the: *definite article*
coast: *noun, common, 3rd person, singular, neuter, accusative case, object to preposition* **along**
in: *preposition governing* **ship**
his: *pronoun, possessive, 3rd person, singular, masculine, genitive case*
small: *adjective qualifying the* **noun**
ship: *noun, common, 3rd person, singular, neuter, accusative case, object to preposition* **in**
Endeavour: *noun, proper, 3rd person, singular, neuter, accusative case, object to preposition* **in**.

PARSING ADVERBIAL COMPOUNDS

Often words which look like prepositions are in fact adverbs. They do not have their own object, i.e. they do not show the relationship of one thing to another, but they compound with other words. We parse them according to the part of speech of the compound which has been formed.

Compounds formed with verbs

    wash up   set to
    carry on   fall over

Please **wash up** the dishes,
verb

They **carried on** with the game.
verb

Compounds formed with nouns

Mostly noun compounds are formed with the adverb in front:

Parsing

outlook   income
offspring   onset

We **tied up** the yacht before the **onset** of the storm.
　　　verb　　　　　　　　　　　　　*noun*

The farmer's **offspring** were **brought up** by the governess.
　　　　　　noun　　　　　*verb*

More noun compounds are coming into use with the adverb following the verb but joined by a hyphen:

lock-up   hand-out
break-in   lay-by

The	two	boys	slept	soundly	under	a	palm	tree.
|	|	|	|	|	|	|	|	|
Definite article	*numeral adjective describing noun 'boys'*	*common noun third person plural masculine nominative case subject of verb 'slept'*	*verb intransitive past simple tense active voice*	*adverb modifying verb 'slept'*	*preposition governing noun 'tree'*	*indefinite article*	*adjective qualifying noun 'tree'*	*common noun third person neuter accusative case object of preposition 'under'*

9
Sentences

A sentence is a group of words expressing at least one complete idea.

Therefore, in order to make sense, a sentence must have at least two parts.

1. A finite verb, with its subject*

subject	finite verb
The baby bird	cheeped.
All the children	laughed.
My brother	is digging.

2. Predicate: All of the sentence which is not the subject is called the predicate.

	predicate	
subject	finite verb	the rest
The chicken	laid	a crooked egg.
The farmer's pretty wife	will use	the crooked egg.
John and Max	have taken	the chicken to the market.
I	hope	you enjoy the pancakes.

SENTENCE STRUCTURE

All sentences are made up of clauses and phrases.

---
* For subjects, see pp. 21-2.

CLAUSE

A clause is a group of words containing a subject and predicate. It must, therefore, contain a finite verb and can form a simple sentence.

>The sun rose.
>The bells rang.
>The boy was bitten.
>Linda fell out of bed.

For more about clauses, see pp. 119-29.

PHRASE

A phrase is a group of words which does not contain a finite verb. Therefore it can be only part of a sentence.

>With a magnet.
>In the sky.
>A wayward boy.

For more about phrases, see pp. 116-18.

KINDS OF SENTENCE

SIMPLE SENTENCE

A sentence must contain one finite verb, that is a verb with a subject.

Every sentence must contain a *principal clause*. So if a sentence has only one subject and one finite verb, then this must be its principal clause. This is sometimes called the independent clause because it can stand alone.

We call this a *Simple Sentence*.

>The bus stopped.
>Everyone jumped off quickly.
>Nina bought a pie.

Sentences

Longer sentences can have more than one finite verb.

    (Mandy **sat** on the gate) while (she **ate** her sandwich)
          finite verb   *finite verb*

Each finite verb is part of a clause. So this means there is more than one clause in the sentence. There is *one* clause for *each* finite verb.

Sentences with more than one clause can be:

compound — two or more principal clauses.

complex — one principal (independent) clause, plus at least one subordinate (dependent) clause.

compound/complex — two or more principal clauses, plus at least one subordinate clause.

COMPOUND SENTENCE

A sentence can have two principal clauses. They are of equal importance and neither clause is dependent on a word in the other clause.

The clauses in compound sentences are usually joined together with and or but.

The bus stopped	and	we all got out.
principal clause	*link*	*principal clause*
Tim likes peanut butter	but	I prefer jam.
principal clause	*link*	*principal clause*
Nina bought a pie	and	ate it quickly.
principal clause	*link*	*principal clause*

COMPLEX SENTENCE

A complex sentence has at least one principal clause and also one or more subordinate clauses.

SUBORDINATE (DEPENDENT) CLAUSES

A subordinate clause is one which is linked in someway to the Principal clause and is dependent on it. It can also be called a dependent clause.

The bus stopped   where   the new road ends.
principal clause   *link*   *subordinate clause*

Where the road ends would not make sense on its own. It is dependent on the principal clause.

Everyone jumped off   although   it was raining.
principal clause   *link*   *subordinate clause*

Nina bought a pie   because   she was hungry.
principal clause   *link*   *subordinate clause*

There are three kinds of subordinate clause. A subordinate clause can do the work of an adjective, an adverb or a noun.

For details of the different kinds of clauses, see pp. 119-29.

COMPOUND COMPLEX SENTENCE

This is a sentence with more than one principal clause and one or more subordinate clauses.

The bus stopped   and   we all jumped out
principal clause 1   *principal clause 2*

where the new road ends.
subordinate clause

Nina bought a pie	and	ate it quickly
principal clause 1		*principal clause 2*

because she was hungry.
subordinate clause

If a sentence is constructed correctly, it can have several clauses and still be clear and easy to understand.

Nina bought a pie	and	ate it quickly
principal clause	*link*	*principal clause*

because	she was hungry	although	she had just had lunch.
link	*subordinate clause*	*link*	*subordinate clause*

The important thing is to remember that each clause must contain a finite verb, and each subordinate clause must be joined by a link word to the clause upon which it is dependent.

When writing, it is better to stick to simple sentences at first, so that your meaning is always clear. With practice you will increase your skill in writing complex sentences, as long as you remember the rules of construction.

For more about clauses and sentence construction, see pp. 119-29.

I sat down	while	I read the book
principal clause	*link*	*subordinate clause*

Exercises – Part One

NOUNS

KINDS OF NOUN

1. Write a list of the things you see on the nearest desk or table. These will mostly be common nouns. If not, what are they?

2. Write down the names of the members of your family. What kind of nouns are these?

3. Name *collective* nouns you could use for groups of the following:
   a. soldiers
   b. people in church
   c. people singing together
   d. people watching a play
   e. actors in a play
   f. people waiting in a line
   g. ships
   h. vehicles moving in a line

4. Divide a page into four columns, headed *common, proper, collective, abstract* and enter each of these nouns under the correct heading:

Exercises – Part One

cave, comfort, piecrust, traffic, St Paul, honey, fear journey, California, prunes, emu, team, orange, Easter, love, tribe, lassie, loss, bunch, greed, Prince Edward

SINGULAR AND PLURAL

5. Fill in the gaps

Singular	Plural
leg	....
dish	....
....	ways
leaf	....
lorry	....
....	berries
weekend	....
sheep	....
....	lunches
ice-cream	....

6. Pick out the nouns in the following sentences. Say whether they are singular or plural.

   The truck drove through the windows of the tax office.
   The notes jangled noisily as the piano crashed down the staircase.

7. Change each singular noun into plural and

8. Change each plural noun into singular.

MASCULINE, FEMININE AND NEUTER

9. Put the following nouns into the right column.
   Masculine   Feminine   Neuter
   boy
   truck, storm, witch, soldier, rubber, maid, goose, mare, airman, apple, pig, princess, stag, horn, youth

POSSESSION

10. Give these people or things one or more possession/s. e.g. David's bike

Lucy, Grandad, my sister, the clock, the girls, Joyce, the cars, his dog, Aunty, the leader, Matilda, the players

PRONOUNS

1. Mark all the *pronouns* in the following sentences:
   a. I did it all by myself.
   b. Whose socks are these?
   c. She had some toffees in her pocket.
   d. That is my programme; this one is yours.
   e. You may share the watermelon he gave us.
   f. Who did this? No-one knows.
   g. He will hand out the cards; each has a number on it.
   h. Somebody take these to the lost property office.
   i. That is the boy who loaded the truck by himself.
   j. Everyone tells me it's true.
2. Can you say what kind each one is?

VERBS

FINITE VERBS

1. Turn the following *infinitives* into *finite* verbs of any tense and use in sentences:
   e.g. to limp   The old man limps; or   He was limping
   to drink
   to stick
   to yell
   to multiply
   to squash
   to sparkle
   to scribble
   to boil
   to dream
   to laugh

Exercises — Part One

2. Add a *noun* to complete these sentences.
   e.g. .... is singing   — Olivia is singing

   .... are banging   .... is snoring

   .... was drinking   .... laughs

   .... dances   .... fell over

   .... will wake up   .... will swim

   .... are drawing   .... is rolling

OBJECTS

3. Mark the *Direct* and *Indirect Objects* in these sentences.
   e.g. He dropped a box of worms on the road.
   Answer: box of worms — Direct object
   a. Please hand me those keys.
   b. We gave our friends pancakes for tea.
   c. Dad killed a snake on the road.
   d. Read this sentence and pick out the objects.

PERSON

4. Rewrite first example paragraph on page 24 ('I opened my eyes . . .') in the third person.

5. Rewrite the second example paragraph on page 24 ('Becky came outside . . .') in the first person.

PARTICIPLES

6. Form a complete sentence using the following:
   flying, arguing, joking, galloping, living, broken, bought, rung, collected, risen

7. What is the past participle of these verbs?
   collapse, drink, deal, falter, hide, feel, bring, lose, sweep, tear

REGULAR AND IRREGULAR VERBS

8. Write the past participles of each of these verbs under headings, regular, irregular:

| weep | drip | dig | strive | float |
| lose | smell | throw | lend | fight |

TENSE

9. a. Pick out the *verbs* in the sentences and name the *tense* of each.

   Sally and I are cooking fish.
   It will be Jack's 21st Birthday on Saturday.
   He always leaves his boots in the doorway.
   We were playing hide and seek in the moonlight.
   You will ring the bell at 8 o'clock.

   b. Rewrite each of the above sentences using a *different tense*.

   c. Mark the *verbs* in each of these sentences: say whether it is *past, present* or *future*.

   Uncle Greg is snoring.
   When will you be cooking dinner?
   Tonight there will be an eclipse of the moon.
   Phyllis drives a semi-trailer.
   Dennis tore his coat on the barbed wire.

   d. Rewrite these *verbs* in the *continuous tense*.

   Rolley rides his motorbike over prickles.
   I shall have my 21st Birthday Party on Saturday.
   Malcolm sings in the shower.
   The vet felt the pony all over for broken bones.
   The Governor will plant a tree on Australia Day.

COMPLEMENT

10. a. Mark the *complements* in these sentences. Say whether they are *nouns* or *adjectives*, *single* words or *phrases*.

    That fellow was a clown in the circus.
    We are not amused.
    This is a good year for peaches.
    The ugly toad turned into a handsome prince.
    I wonder who will be our next Prime Minister.

b. Add complements to the following:

These balloons . . . .

Disrespect . . . .

All men . . . .

Industry . . . .

Rubber bands . . . .

c. Mark the complements in the following paragraph:
This hall is a striking building. It is built from the finest sandstone blocks, which were quarried nearby. The builder made a donation of these bricks because he is a very public spirited man. The hall was built for the local community and they are already making good use of it. They are very proud of their hall because it will be a great asset to their social activities.

ADJECTIVES

1. a. Mark the *adjectives* in the following story.
   The moon was full and bright by now, and they could see the land of Green Ginger quite clearly. It was sprinkled with Ginger trees laden down with branch upon branch of sparkling sugar-coated Green Ginger and bright beauteous flowers grew all over the soft velvety grass, and water lilies floated on the cheerful little hubble-bubbling stream. (*The Land of Green Ginger* by Noel Langley)

   b. Draw a line from the *adjective* to the *noun* it qualifies.

   c. Try reading the passage leaving out the adjectives.

   d. What difference does it make?

2. Suggest colourful *adjectives* for these nouns.

   eagle   sea
   dress   supper
   road   donkey
   music   truck
   quarrel   medicine

Exercises — Part One

3. Qualify the *nouns* in this story and see how interesting you can make it.

   She sat by the river dangling her toes among the weeds and watching the sunlight shining on the water. She threw crumbs to the fish delighting in their antics. Suddenly, shadows fell across the water and she realized that clouds had gathered. She felt the first drop of rain on her cheek as she ran through the grass to the gate at the bottom of the garden. It was good to be back in the house again.

4. a. Form adjectives from the following words

   cheer, hope, fear, loathe, thank, lone, love, move, resist, sense, mean

   b. Make sentences using the words you have formed.

5. Fill in the gaps.

Positive	Comparative	Superlative
....	uglier	....
plain	....	....
....	....	driest
....	more complicated	....
....	less	....
tiny	....	....
....	....	bald
trustworthy	....	....
....	funnier	....
....	....	worst

6. Fill in the space in the following sentences:

   a. How old is Val? Are you .... than she is? Then Dan must be the ....

   b. Jess is beautiful. She is .... than Ruth or Helen.

   c. Of you three boys who has .... money?

   d. Which do you like ...., gold or silver?

e. Some of these logs are heavy. Put the .... ones onto the truck.

ADVERBS

1. Mark the *adverbs*.

    a. Jim shouted rudely at the umpire.

    b. Dawn wept bitterly.

    c. They danced wildly to the music.

    d. We all ran fast to the car park.

    e. You can't be too careful.

2. a. Change these *adjectives* into *adverbs*.

    | smart | lazy |
    | loud | loose |
    | wise | pretty |
    | foolish | false |
    | good | contented |

    b. Use each one in a sentence.

PREPOSITIONS

1. Make *prepositional* phrases with these words.

    | through | between |
    | into | beyond |
    | underneath | beneath |

2. Mark the *prepositions* in this passage.

    On Friday, Trudi was walking home from school when she got a stone in her shoe, so she sat down in the middle of the road to remove it. She was shaking her shoe above her head, when suddenly she heard the sound of a vehicle coming round the corner and roaring towards her. She leapt into the air and shoe in hand jumped across the drain and onto the kerb — just in time ....
    'Whew!' She gasped with relief, as she clambered through the fence behind the house, 'That is the last time I shall sit in the road without a shoe.'

ARTICLES, CONJUNCTIONS AND INTERJECTIONS

1. Fill the spaces with a suitable *article*.
    a. Have you got . . . . handkerchief?
    b. Where did you put . . . . screwdriver?
    c. Please pass . . . . butter.
    d. Where are . . . . shoelaces.
    e. May I have . . . . orange?
    f. There's a cockroach in . . . . carton.
    g. You'll find . . . . First Aid Kit in . . . . changing room.
    h. Load . . . . boxes onto . . . . truck.
    i. We had such . . . . adventure on our holidays.
    j. I bought . . . . wheelbarrow at the store on . . . . corner of . . . . street.

2. Join the two parts of a sentence with a suitable *conjunction*.
    a. We sang songs . . . . our throats were sore.
    b. Dad can't put his shoe on . . . . his foot is swollen.
    c. Please change your clothes . . . . you go out.
    d. We enjoyed our trip . . . . the car broke down.
    e. Ultralights are noisy . . . . you don't wear earplugs.
    f. Formula One motor racing has stimulated worldwide interest . . . . it costs a lot of money and involves heavy risks.
    g. We climbed the mountain . . . . get a view of the city spread out below.

PARSING

1. Write the correct part of speech under each word of these sentences.
    a. Phil left his dirty shoes at the door.

Exercises – Part One

b. There is a huge black spider in your desk.
c. A family of ducks crossed the road in front of the car.
d. A helicopter hovered near my hotel balcony.
e. The farmer's wife cut off their tails with the carving knife.
f. Huge uneven hailstones covered the ground.
g. Craig kicked the ball straight between the posts.
h. Suddenly I was swept into the sea by a giant wave.
i. I managed to get my luggage onto the correct flight.
j. The superb open scenery of the Ranges contrasts dramatically with the magnificent world within the forests.

KINDS OF SENTENCES

1. How many clauses are there in each of the following sentences? Underline the *finite verbs* and bracket the *clauses*.

    a. The bus will come past at 4.30.
    b. Firemen broke in and helped us crawl out.
    c. He fed the fish in the pond with the crumbs.
    d. We always have a party when Uncle Tim comes.
    e. There came a big spider and sat down beside her.
    f. Your teeth will fall out if you forget to clean them.
    g. Hannibal crossed the Alps with a herd of elephants.
    h. He opened the door but was forced back by the smoke.
    i. When the cyclone hit we had to hold mattresses over the smashed windows.
    j. Several cruise boats went past but none of them saw us.

    Can you say what kind of sentence each one is, *simple*, *compound* or *complex*?

2. Turn the following into *complex* sentences by adding a *subordinate clause* — remember the addition may go before or after.

a. Bonny screamed.
b. The door flew open.
c. Stop the car!
d. He picked up a stick.
e. They waved goodbye.
f. It vanished into thin air.
g. I got twenty-eight runs.
h. We ran as fast as we could.
i. The camera rolled down the stony slope.
j. It was a very difficult climb.

Part Two
Punctuation

10   Capital letters

11   The full stop

12   The comma

13   The question mark

14   The exclamation mark

15   Inverted commas

16   The apostrophe

17   The semicolon

18   The colon

19   Parentheses and dashes

10
Capital letters

The first rule we learn about writing correctly is that capital letters must be used at the beginning of proper nouns.

    Joshua   Dan
    Jane   Mark

I is always capitalised.

    I like Jane.

Capital letters must be used at the beginning of the first word of every sentence.

    Most people like bananas.
    Where are your socks?
    A spider has eight legs.

A capital letter is used at the beginning of each main word of the title of a book, a film, a person, a play, etc.

    I Can Jump Puddles
    The Secret Garden
    Prince Charles

Note: Articles, conjunctions and prepositions in a title do not need capital letters except to start the first word.
> *William in Trouble*
> *The Land of Green Ginger*
> *Your Worship*
> *The Cat in the Hat*

A capital letter is used at the beginning of a spoken sentence in direct speech even though it follows a comma:
> Jemima cried, 'We'll never see Father and Mother again.'

Note: If the sentence in direct speech is broken, a capital letter does not follow the comma.
> 'It is dangerous,' she warned, 'to wander in the bush alone.'

She called out to Woody, 'Where are you?'

Capital letters are used at the start of a sentence to indicate a proper noun and to introduce direct speech.

11
The full stop

•

AT THE END OF A SENTENCE

Every complete sentence, whether it is short or long, must end with a full stop or a question mark or an exclamation mark.

If the sentence is a statement it will end with a full stop:
> Yes.
> I think so.
> Good books cost a lot of money.
> Chitty Chitty Bang Bang raced along at one hundred miles an hour.

IN ABBREVIATIONS

When a word is abbreviated only part of it is written. It is a shortened form. A full stop shows that the other part of the word is missing:
> We have only ten sq. cm. of card left.
> Send this letter to Capt. Johns.
> This story to be cont. next week.

When the initials are used instead of whole words, a full stop is used after each one.

The full stop

P.T.O.   (Please Turn Over).
R.S.V.P. Repondez S'il Vous Plait. (please reply).
M.B.E.   Member (of the order of the) British Empire.
N.S.W.   New South Wales.

Note: It is now acceptable to omit full stops, particularly when the shortened form of the word ends with the same letter as the word itself:

Mr   Mister
Dr   Doctor
dept department

Whether you choose to use full stops or not, it is essential to be consistent and follow the same style throughout the one piece of writing.

12
The comma
,

It is harder to describe when commas should be used as it often depends on the way that the sentence should be spoken or read.

PAUSE

A comma indicates a pause which makes the sense of the sentence clear. Often in speech the pitch of the voice is raised on the last word before the comma:

> Lorette, the last runner in, had blisters all over her feet.

Note: The pitch of the voice is usually lowered at the end of the statement:

> Although he was sick, he did not go home.
> The lion, with the antelope in its jaws, jumped clean over the fence.

DIRECT SPEECH

Commas are used to 'mark off' direct speech:

> 'When I get home,' Dick moaned, 'I shall go to bed.'

They also indicate where pauses occur:
>Although he was sick, he did not go home.
>The lion, with the antelope in its jaws, jumped clean over the fence.

Commas help the reader to read correctly and with expression.

13
The question mark
?

A question mark is used instead of a full stop at the end of any kind of question; that is, when the speaker wants the answer to something he is asking:

>Who did this?
>Where are you?
>Why did the bull rush?

and in direct speech in narrative:

>Mother asked, 'Whatever have you done to your shirt?'
>'Why didn't you call the police?' the man cried.

Note: As with commas, voice pitch is raised on the last word of a question.

Question marks are not used when indirect speech is used.

>Uncle Reg asked whether the bus stopped at the bridge.
>The teacher inquired how many boys were going on the school outing.

Note: The voice is lowered on the last word of the sentence in reported speech.

14
The exclamation mark
!

This mark is used at the end of a sentence spoken suddenly or loudly expressing surprise or shock:
> You confounded idiot!
> Heavens!
> Whatever next!

or to express strong feelings such as anger, fear or despair:
> 'Take that bone outside!' Dad yelled at the dog.
> He's caught in the weeds!
> Help!
> Alas! It was too late!

Sometimes exclamations can look like questions, but the speaker is not seeking an answer.

If you are not sure whether the sentence is a question or not, you can ask yourself whether the speaker is trying to find something out. If he is, then it is a question:
> How many cards do we need?
> What work did he do?

The exclamation mark

If the speaker is not seeking an answer, then the sentence is an exclamation:

> What a rude boy!
> Can you beat it!
> Isn't he clever!

Yuk!

An interjection; the exclamation mark indicates the strength of feeling.

15
Inverted commas
" "

Some people call these the sixes and nines, to remember which comes first.

Inverted commas enclose or "mark off" the actual words that somebody says:

'I saw your picture in the paper,' said Ruby.
'What is that on your shoe?' asked Julie.

Anything not spoken cannot be included inside the inverted commas, so they sometimes have to be closed and opened again:

'Hang on', shouted the pilot, 'I am on my way.'
'I know, I know,' called Philip, putting up his hand, 'It's the equator.'

All other punctuation marks coming at the end of a sentence must be included inside the inverted commas.

'What a nasty mess!' Andrew cried.

Notice that the exclamation mark or question mark in direct speech replaces a comma.

'Who is that man?' asked Jenny.

but:
> 'He is my Uncle,' answered Kelly.

NAMES AND TITLES

In books, magazines, etc other forms of print are used (eg italics) for titles of films, books, poems, etc, but when we are writing we can mark them with inverted commas:

> Have you read 'Blinky Bill' yet?
> We saw 'Fire and Ice' on T.V. yesterday.
> 'Bagdad Cafe' is a fantastic film.
> 'The Man from Snowy River' was written by Banjo Patterson.

16
The apostrophe
,

An apostrophe *shows* that somebody or something *owns* something.

The apostrophe follows the person or thing that owns it.

SINGULAR

After a single noun we add s

>Kevin's shirt is wet.
>The cat's collar fell off.
>My daughter's friend won the prize.
>Alf did his brother's homework.
>We love Mum's apple pie.

Note: If a word already ends in s and another one makes it sound clumsy, the s can be left off but the apostrophe stays:

>For Jesus' sake.
>Stiggins' bakery

PLURAL

If the noun is plural, the apostrophe still comes after the name of the people or things that own something:

The apostrophe

The boys' football split open.
You can swim in the men's pool today.
The party will be at the Parkes' house.
They are playing in the Jones' yard.

or

They are playing in the Joneses' yard.

Note
1. If two people or more own something only the last one has the apostrophe ending:
   It is in Pat and Jane**'s** room
   This is Rod, Lucy and Jennifer**'s** lunch.

2. Sometimes something is available for a certain group of people; it does not belong to them, so it is acting as an adjective and does not have an apostrophe:
   Students Union
   Teachers handbook
   Writers Journal.

MISSING LETTERS

An apostrophe is used to show when and where a letter or letters have been left out. This can make two words become one:

It is a lovely day.	It's a lovely day.
When is the next match?	When's the next match?
I have a good idea.	I've a good idea.
They are always late.	They're always late.
They could have gone.	They could've gone.

PLURALS OF NUMBERS AND LETTERS

To make the sense clear, apostrophes are sometimes used in the plurals of numbers and letters, especially in handwriting:

> He was born in the 1960's.
> How many s's in that word?
> There are four 4's in her number.
> Mind your p's and q's.

SEE THE DIFFERENCE!

Yours, ours, theirs do not have apostrophes as they are either possessive pronouns or adjectives.

When its is a pronoun meaning 'owned by it', it does not have an apostrophe either:

Look at **its** cage. *possessive adjective*	But	**It's** a cage. **(It is)**
This boat is **theirs**.	But	**There's** my boat. **(There is)**
Their son is a pilot.	But	**They're** in the garden. **(They are)**
Your train has gone! *possessive*	But	**You're** too late! **(You are)**
Whose lunch is this? *possessive adjective*	But	**Who's** having lunch? **(Who is)**

17
The semicolon

;

A semicolon separates two complete ideas which could be written in two separate sentences; they are written in one sentence to show that they are very closely connected.

Usually the second idea is an extension of the first part, or an addition to it.

A semicolon is not half a colon; it has a job of its own.

> The DC9 crashed on landing; it overshot the runway.
> We should go home now; it would be impolite to stay.

Sometimes it is used to separate lines of poetry:

> 'Wishes of an Elderly Man' *Sir Walter Raleigh*
>
> I wish I loved the Human Race;
> I wish I loved its silly face;
> I wish I liked the way it walks;
> I wish I liked the way it talks;
> And when I'm introduced to one
> I wish I thought *What Jolly Fun!*

Sometimes semicolons are used for lists where a longer pause is required than that provided by a comma:

> Write a sentence using the following words: image; colour; matter; energy.

> Goods for auction were arranged on the tables: boxes of odd plates and dishes; bundles of assorted cutlery; stacks of outdated records and old-fashioned dress patterns; piles of used piping mixed with rusty garden tools.

The conjurer pulled many things out of the hat: the odd rabbit or two; several silk scarves; a rather scruffy dove; and numerous assorted guinea pigs.

18
The colon

:

The colon is another kind of stop, less strong than a full stop. It is mostly used for a special purpose: It shows that a list or illustration is to come:

> Items stolen from the house included: fine gold rings, two pearl brooches, several pairs of cufflinks and a diamond necklace. There are eight parts of speech: Nouns, verb, pronouns, adjectives, adverbs, prepositions, conjunctions and articles.

The colon is useful in making notes or giving instructions:

> Reasons for oiling your bicycle:
> 1. To protect moving parts.
> 2. To prevent rust from forming.
> 3. To keep out dust.
> 4. To make it shine.

Sometimes a colon is used before a quotation:

> Edward Lear wrote: 'It's a fact the whole world knows, that Pobbles are happier without their toes.'

19
Parentheses and dashes
( )   —

PARENTHESES

Parentheses (or brackets) are used to enclose an addition, usually telling the reader a little more about something mentioned before the parentheses.

Notice that the sentence must still make sense even if the part in parentheses is left out:

> Mary was born two months (and two days, to be exact) before her father came back.
>
> We usually go to Dickinsons (the camera shop in Roth Street) to get our films developed.

Sometimes the parentheses serve to remind the reader of a fact:

> The leader of the team (Ben Collins), Joseph Smart and Lew Edwards were present. (*NB*: Without the parentheses it might seem that the leader of the team and Ben Collins were separate people.)
>
> I have decided to go to Tamworth (my favourite inland town) for the Country Music Festival.
>
> Jack drove all night (silly idiot) to get here in time for the races.

DASHES

Dashes are also used for an addition, but there is a small, subtle difference between additions in parentheses and addition between dashes. Most people choose which to use instinctively.

Additions between parentheses usually add more explanation or description of what went before.

Additions between dashes are often extra complete ideas, indicating the speaker's own thoughts about something mentioned in the sentence.

> We went to the rodeo on Saturday — not that I like rodeos, but Jim does — and guess whom I met there?
>
> Rosy and Phil had a conjuror — a real one I mean, hired from the city — at their party last night.
>
> He gave me a lovely rose — yes, a single red one — after the performance.

Exercises – Part Two

CAPITAL LETTERS

1. Rewrite these sentences with capitals where they should be.

    a. in the christmas holidays we went to dreamland, but at easter we are going to disneyland in america.

    b. hayley lewis won five gold medals at the commonwealth games.

    c. john travolta was born on 18 February 1954; do you know when jason donovan was born?

    d. sandy took his new book *charlie and the chocolate factory* to school to show to mr kennedy.

    e. dad reads the *daily sun*, mum reads her *women's weekly* but i like the comic strips especially tom and jerry.

PUNCTUATION MARKS

1. Rewrite these sentences using correct punctuation marks:

    a. one passenger jumped out just before the plane dived

    b. jump jump we are going to crash

Exercises – Part Two

c. did you see where the plane landed

d. wow they are lucky to be alive

e. shaken but unhurt he scrambled to his feet

f. the parachute which had saved his life lay limp and torn across the stubble

g. ben do you ever think you will go flying again

h. of course danny but i have learned from the experience

i. parts of the plane tail undercarriage seat and propeller were strewn all over the paddock

j. the plane was a wreck but oh boy you should see Ben's new one – a cessna 120.

INVERTED COMMAS

1. Punctuate the following sentences correctly using inverted commas:

   a. Why didn't you come to my party asked Des.

   b. I had promised to go to Damions party replied Belinda didn't you get my reply.

   c. No did you send one answered Des I was expecting you to turn up.

   d. Sorry answered Belinda I wish I had come to yours instead.

   e. You missed a good night Belinda called Phil through the window never mind come inside and join us.

   f. Belinda stepped inside followed by Des Whew it's hot in here she cried can we open some windows.

   g. Yes do called mum from the kitchen I was trying to keep out the insects while I was cooking.

   h. Don't worry laughed Des we all like squashed fly cake don't we girls.

i. Well if you behave yourselves you can have some of the squashed fly cake said mum handing out a try there you are boys and girls.

j. Oh Mrs Randall what a super cake burst out Belinda with her mouth full would you let me have the recipe.

THE APOSTROPHE

1. Where would you put the apostrophe?
    a. We are going swimming in Lindas pool.
    b. Ask Ken to bring Nevs floatie.
    c. The girls have got Mums watch.
    d. Kens pool is better than ours.
    e. My aunts pool always has leaves in the bottom and green round the sides.

2. a. My togs are slipping down. I'll have to go and borrow Julies.
    b. I'm wearing my sisters togs because hers fit me better.
    c. Hello Ken have you got Nevs floatie? Are they Nevs goggles too?
    d. No. They are Lindas. Where are yours? Lindas were under Mums bag.
    e. Where is Mums watch? We have to be at Uncle Dicks for tea remember. This is his birthday.

3. a. Tom Jule lives around here. Is this the Jules house with the red tiles?
    b. I brought Dads mower here on St. Patricks Day so he could mow old Toms lawn.
    c. I like Sam Jules motorbike. Its an expensive Harley-Davidson like Mike Turners.
    d. Have you seen Mike Turners bike gear? He goes to all the rallies with Sam Jules sister.
    e. Are they all the Jules motorbikes lined up in that shed next to Mrs Jules car?

Exercises – Part Two

4. Fill in the spaces with one of the following: its, it is, it has.

    a. .... a lovely day. Let's go to the zoo.

    b. Look at the elephant. .... got something in .... trunk.

    c. .... a bun. Look at .... baby .... only a month old.

    d. .... funny how the baby strokes .... mother's leg with .... trunk.

    e. .... hungry .... looking for .... feed.

    f. I wonder if .... feeding time for the lions yet.

    g. Oh look at that meat .... getting for .... dinner.

    h. I think .... our dinnertime too, but I don't fancy sharing .... meat.

    i. .... meat is probably very tasty but .... better cooked.

    j. .... better in a hamburger. There's a cafe. Let's see if .... open; oh yes .... got a menu inside .... door.

5. Write the word with the apostrophe as two words:
   e.g. It's too late. Write as It is too late.

    a. I'm freezing cold.

    b. Haven't you got a jacket?

    c. I've left it behind.

    d. You're a silly fellow.

    e. He's left his at home too!

6. Use an apostrophe to make two words one:

    a. Where have they gone? They did not tell me.

    b. They are getting some food. I hope they have some money.

    c. I should like to go too. Can I not go?

d. You are too late now. You should have gone with them.

e. When will they get back? I am hungry.

7. Write out the following sentence in full.

She'd've liked to've gone to see Starlight Express, but she couldn't because she'd 'flu, so if you'll get her a ticket when you're in town she'll be able to go when she's better.

THE SEMICOLON AND THE COLON

Use semicolons and colons to:

1. Describe the goods you can find in a secondhand shop.
2. List the tasks for the kitchen cleaner.
3. List the benefits of city life.
4. List the advantages of air travel and transport.

PARENTHESES AND DASHES

1. Add brackets and dashes where you think they should go in the following sentences.

    a. Lucy had a cold she always gets colds so we had to stay at home.

    b. I think I might take a nap hey I've missed my dental appointment.

    c. Here Mel take these plates they're Mum's best ones to the kitchen.

    d. I er thought you might be asleep.

    e. I didn't want to don't be silly.

    f. She gave me the change fourteen shillings and sixpence to put into the cash box.

    g. Try writing a book a really good book like *My Cousin, Rachel*.

    h. Put this up on the light's gone out!

    i. Edwin the choir leader has got engaged.

    j. You should see his ring very expensive.

Part Three
More about verbs

20 Transitive and intransitive

21 Voice: active and passive

22 Perfect tenses

23 Emphatic tenses

24 Participles as adjectives

25 Participles as nouns (gerunds)

26 Mood

20
Verbs: transitive and intransitive

TRANSITIVE AND INTRANSITIVE VERBS

Transitive means 'crossing' or 'passing over'. The action of a transitive verb crosses or passes over to a direct object.

　　　Uncle Rex **bought** a new **motor bike**.

　　　Geoff **kicked** a **goal**.

　　　Maureen never **eats meat**.

　　　We **watched** a **video** last night.

If it makes sense when you say 'something' after the verb (or 'anything' if your sentence is negative) then the verb must be transitive.

　　　Uncle Rex bought something.
　　　What did he buy?
　　　Answer: *a motor bike.*

The verb bought is therefore transitive.

An intransitive verb does *not* take an object.

　　　The sun shines.
　　　The old boat was drifting.
　　　Dad laughed till he cried.

Try adding something after these verbs —
> The sun shines something . . .

This does not make sense, so in this sentence shines is intransitive.

Note: Some verbs can be transitive or intransitive:
> The sun **shines**.
> *intransitive*

but
> Dad **shines** his **shoes**.

Shines has an object, so it is transitive.

Mara   cooked   pancakes
transitive verb
common noun object of the transitive verb 'cooked'

21
Voice: active and passive

ACTIVE

The verb is said to be in the active voice when the *subject* of the verb is the *doer* of the action.

    Nancy **threw** the ball.
    Tim **cooked** pancakes.
    The car **rolled** down the bank.

PASSIVE

The verb is called *passive* when its subject has the action done to him/her/it.

    Nancy **was hit** by the ball.
    John **was taken** to hospital in the ambulance.
    The car **was polished** by Greg.
    We **were drenched** by the downpour.

22
Perfect tenses

The past participle is used to show an action which is completed, or perfect.
      eaten, ridden, swum

Therefore we use the past participle to make perfect tenses. Auxiliary verbs must be added to complete the tense:

PRESENT PERFECT (sometimes called the Perfect)

The auxiliary is in the present tense. The action is completed now.

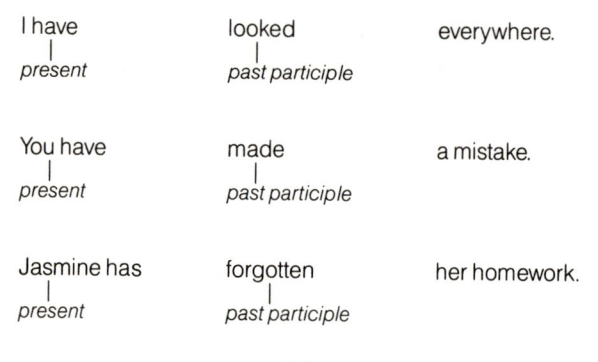

    I have   looked   everywhere.
     | |
   present   *past participle*

    You have   made   a mistake.
     | |
   present   *past participle*

    Jasmine has   forgotten   her homework.
     | |
   present   *past participle*

Perfect tenses

PAST PERFECT (sometimes called the Pluperfect)

The auxiliary is in the past tense. The action was completed some time in the past.

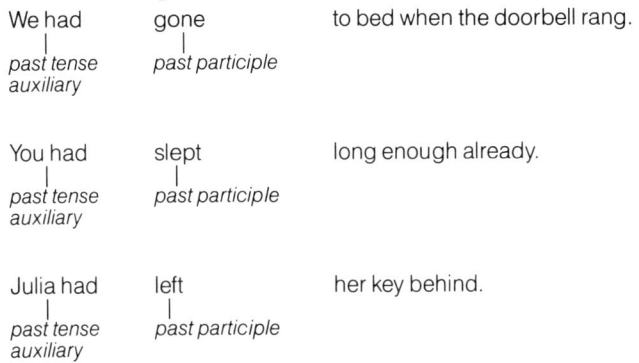

| We had | gone | to bed when the doorbell rang. |
| *past tense auxiliary* | *past participle* | |

| You had | slept | long enough already. |
| *past tense auxiliary* | *past participle* | |

| Julia had | left | her key behind. |
| *past tense auxiliary* | *past participle* | |

FUTURE PERFECT

The auxiliary is in the future tense. The action will have been completed at some time in the future.

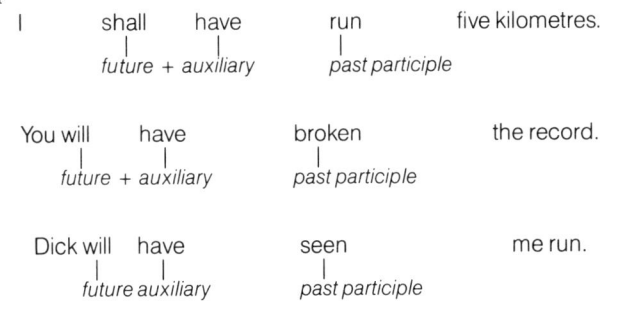

| I shall have | run | five kilometres. |
| *future + auxiliary* | *past participle* | |

| You will have | broken | the record. |
| *future + auxiliary* | *past participle* | |

| Dick will have | seen | me run. |
| *future auxiliary* | *past participle* | |

TENSES REGULAR

ACTIVE VOICE

Singular Person	Present	Past	Future
1st	I laugh	I laughed	I shall laugh
2nd	You laugh	You laughed	You will laugh
3rd	He/she/it laughs	He/she/it laughed	He/she/it will laugh

Plural Person			
1st	We laugh	We laughed	We shall laugh
2nd	You laugh	You laughed	You will laugh
3rd	They laugh	They laughed	They will laugh

Singular Person	Present Perfect	Past Perfect	Future Perfect
1st	I have laughed	I had laughed	I shall have laughed
2nd	You have laughed	You had laughed	You will have laughed
3rd	He/she/it has laughed	He/she/it had laughed	He/she/it will have laughed

Plural Person			
1st	We have laughed	We had laughed	We shall have laughed
2nd	You have laughed	You had laughed	You will have laughed
3rd	They have laughed	They had laughed	They will have laughed

PASSIVE VOICE

Singular Person	Present	Past	Future
1st	I am painted	I was painted	I shall be painted
2nd	You are painted	You were painted	You will be painted
3rd	He/she it is painted	He/she/it was painted	He/she/it will be painted

Plural Person			
1st	We are painted	We were painted	We shall be painted
2nd	You are painted	You were painted	You will be painted
3rd	They are painted	They were painted	They will be painted

Singular Person	Present Perfect	Past Perfect	Future Perfect
1st	I have been painted	I had been painted	I shall have been painted
2nd	You have been painted	You had been painted	You will have been painted
3rd	He/she/it has been painted	He/she/it had been painted	He/she/it will have been painted

Plural Person			
1st	We have been painted	We had been painted	We shall have been painted
2nd	You have been painted	You had been painted	You will have been painted
3rd	They have been painted	They had been painted	They will have been painted

23
Emphatic tenses

To give emphasis, the verb to do is used as the auxiliary, in the present and past tenses:

PRESENT

    I **do** love the bush!
    You **do** look pretty!
    Tania **does** put on airs!

PAST

    We **did** have a problem!
    You **did** do a good job!
    They **did** drive carefully!

FUTURE

To give emphasis using a future tense we invert the auxiliary forms will and shall.

Emphatic tenses

I/we shall	becomes	I/we **will**
you will	becomes	you **shall**
he/she/it will	becomes	he/she/it **shall**

I	**will**	go.
You	**shall**	pay for it.
It	**shall**	be done.
They	**shall**	apologise.

24
Participles as verbs and adjectives

Participles are very flexible because they can be different parts of speech according to the work that they do in the sentence.

PARTICIPLES ACTING AS VERBS

As we have seen, both present and past participles are used with auxiliary verbs to form complete tenses.

The Queen Mother is smiling.
present participle

The soldier has ridden home.
past participle

PARTICIPLES ACTING AS ADJECTIVES

If a participle is telling you more about a noun, that is, qualifying the noun, then it is an adjective.

A **smiling** Sally collected her prize.

Present Participle

> The **chanting** throng marched towards the city.
> She was known as the **singing** nun.
> They watched the **breaking** rope in horror.
> The children love the **moving** staircase.

Past Participle

> He cut himself with the **broken** knife.
> We shall read about the **lost** empire.
> You should try my **toasted** marshmallows.
> He carried a **sawn-off** shot gun.
> We all drink **pasteurised** milk.

A	laughing	boy made coffee with	boiled	water.
	present participle used as an adjective qualifying the noun 'boy'		*past participle used as an adjective qualifying the noun 'water'*	

25
Participles as nouns (gerunds)

If a present participle is used as a subject, an object, or governed by a preposition, then it is a noun.
We call this a gerund.

GERUND — as subject
    Swimming is fine exercise.
    Canoeing requires strength and skill.
    Dropping a match could start a fire.
    Cooking destroys vitamins.

GERUND — as object
    Joyce loves **gardening**.
    This blouse needs **ironing**.
    Pilots practise **circling** the runway.
    Some firms prohibit **smoking** on the premises.

GERUND — governed by preposition, that is, object of a preposition. (See p. 38.)

Participles as nouns (gerunds)

He is skilled in **wood-chopping**.
Here is some bait for **fishing**.
I am tired of **waiting**.
On **hearing** the news, he collapsed.

Swotting   leaves a lot to be desired.
|
*gerund
subject
of verb
'leaves'*

26
Mood

Mood shows the *form* of the action of the verb.

IMPERATIVE — Command

This mood is used for expressing commands or orders:
>**Present** Arms!
>**Stop** at the red light.
>Please **leave** your boots outside.
>Those in favour **raise** your hands.

INDICATIVE — Statement or Question

The indicative mood expresses a statement of fact, or a question.
>Worms **are** good for fishing.
>Do you **like** fishing?
>Jack Sprat **ate** no fat.
>Who **knows** how to make pumpkin scones?

SUBJUNCTIVE — Doubt

This mood is for expressing some thing which is not definite, but is uncertain, doubtful or hypothetical.

If I **were** you, I **would keep** a diary.
Should the baker call, you **can buy** a loaf.
You **would be** wise to leave in a hurry.
May all your dreams **come** true!

Dithering may not pay dividends.

Exercises — Part Three

TRANSITIVE AND INTRANSITIVE

1. Pick out the verbs in the passage and say whether each one is *transitive* or *intransitive*. You could write them in two columns.

   John slipped on his jacket and hurried out. He jumped onto his bike and pedalled happily down the street. He sang his favourite tune, too, because it was the first day of the holidays and he had exciting plans. The sun shone, a breeze softly blew and John was going camping. Firstly, he called into the Disposals Store and bought some more tent pegs and a powerful torch. His aunt had given him some money for his Birthday, so he splashed out on a string hammock that could double as a carry bag or even a fishing net. Life was good, and he smiled with joyful anticipation as he left the shop and pedalled home again to pack his gear for the great adventure.

VOICE: ACTIVE AND PASSIVE

1. Write these sentences in the *passive* voice.

    a. Darcy knocked the vase over.

    b. Maggie ate a whole bowl of sugared almonds.

Exercises – Part Three

    c. Helmut let the huge dog off its chain.

    d. We used all the string on the cubby house.

    e. Max will ring you in the morning.

    f. The falling branch hit him on the head.

    g. Mum burnt the dinner when she answered the door.

    h. He left the trailer on jacks all night.

    i. You can chop down that tree in the morning.

    j. They laid the tarmac and rolled the road.

2. Write these sentences in the *active* voice.

    a. This thatched house was built in the nineteenth century.

    b. Lengths of grass are cut into convenient handfuls by the thatchers.

    c. The binder knot is used for the purpose.

    d. Long sticks are threaded through the bunches.

    e. These are wired onto the rafters or supported by wooden pegs.

    f. Each layer is prepared on the ground and then lifted into place.

    g. The house was kept very cool by the thatched roof.

    h. When tribal huts are built, interlocking forked sticks are buried in the ground.

    i. Provisions are kept for long periods by bush dwellers in huts with mud floors which are wetted every morning.

    j. Every year the huts are damaged by the heavy rains and repaired again before the next season.

PERFECT TENSES

1. Fill in the correct *participle*.

    a. I have (leave) my ticket at home.

- b. We have (go) to fetch it.
- c. He has (drive) the taxi quickly.
- d. We have (pay) the taxi driver.
- e. I have (bring) my ticket.
- f. They have (hurry) to the airport.
- g. The plane has (take off).
- h. They have (gasp) in horror.
- i. We have (make) a new booking.

2. Change the following into *Perfect* tenses.
    - a. We shall go to the show four times.
    - b. He forgot his lunch.
    - c. The baby panda was very sick.
    - d. Who rode on the donkey?
    - e. The bumper cars kept breaking down.
    - f. The man's glasses fall off.
    - g. I spend all my money.
    - h. We had a wonderful day.
    - i. The horse broke the fence.
    - j. Lucy will catch cold without her jacket.

3. Can you name the tense?
    - a. They brought our relocatable home yesterday.
    - b. We are looking forward to moving in.
    - c. They had left the factory before dawn.
    - d. The carpets will be laid in the morning.
    - e. They were welding the rails for the steps.
    - f. Those men do work hard!

Exercises – Part Three

g. The lorry has gone to collect some cement.

h. They will pour it into the holes.

i. I hope they won't spill it.

j. They will have broken two windows.

k. What a lovely house!

PARTICIPLES

1. Pick out the *participles* from the passage.

   Young Luke was lost. He had ridden his bicycle from home and was thinking so hard about his new plans that he had forgotten to take the turning past the church. Suddenly, he noticed a fallen tree, lying across the path ahead. The broken branches were strewn in all directions. Luke was worried and excited all at once; he had found a new secret place for climbing and exploring with his friend Rick. Turning he searched for the track he had followed; the setting sun was dazzling his eyes. Bewildered he realised that darkness had suddenly fallen and he was beaten. Being lost is always daunting even for the most experienced traveller.

2. Fill in the space with a suitable *participle*.

   a. The . . . . lion frightened the keeper.

   b. . . . . and white they led him to the waiting car.

   c. . . . . wood fetches a high price.

   d. We waved goodbye to the . . . . boys.

   e. Collect the . . . . pieces and put them on the desk.

   f. . . . . keeps you fit.

   g. . . . . children climbed into the bus.

   h. The bin was full of . . . . mangos.

   i. Flyn jumped off the . . . . train.

   j. The . . . . girl handed her brother the . . . . parcel.

Name the part of speech of each of your chosen participles.

Part Four

Sentences: more about clauses and phrases

27 Case

28 Phrases

29 Clauses

30 Sentence analysis

27
Case

Case is very simple to understand. The part that a noun or pronoun plays in its clause gives it its case. Understanding case is very important when learning a foreign language.

There are five cases in English.

NOMINATIVE CASE

The subject of a verb is in the nominative case:

> **I** love sausages!
> *Subject*
> *Nominative Case*

> **The sausages** are ready.
> *Subject*
> *Nominative Case*

> **They** forgot the tomato sauce.
> *Subject*
> *Nominative Case*

ACCUSATIVE CASE

The Direct Object of a sentence is in the Accusative Case:

> We love **furry animals.**
> *Direct Object*
> *Accusative Case*

> He loves **me.**
> *Direct Object*
> *Accusative Case*

Everyone loves **someone.**
　　　　　　Direct Object
　　　　　　Accusative Case

DATIVE CASE

The Indirect Object of a sentence forms the Dative Case:

　　Tell **us**　　　　a story
　　　　Indirect Object
　　　　Dative Case

　　Uncle John gave **Dawn**　　a dollar.
　　　　　　　　Indirect Object
　　　　　　　　Dative Case

　　Janelle wrote **me**　　a letter.
　　　　　Indirect Object
　　　　　Dative Case

　　We sent **her**　　a bunch of flowers.
　　　Indirect Object
　　　Dative Case

GENITIVE (possessive) CASE

Someone or something possessing something forms the Genitive Case:

　　Dick's　　mail is late.
　　Possessor
　　Genitive Case

　　Greg ate **Crystal's**　　sandwich.
　　　　　Possessor
　　　　　Genitive Case

　　They all went to **her**　　house.
　　　　　　Possesssor
　　　　　　Genitive Case

But I went home to clean **Dad's** car.
                                Possessor
                                Genitive Case

VOCATIVE CASE

A word used for calling (or addressing) someone is in the Vocative Case:

    Go home, **Gerry.**
            Person addressed
            Vocative Case

    Waiter, please bring the menu.
    Person addressed
    Vocative Case

    Are you feeling better, **son?**
                        Person addressed
                        Vocative Case

    Look, **Sir,** I've finished.
        Person addressed
        Vocative Case

NOUNS AND PRONOUNS IN DIFFERENT CASES

The following examples show nouns and pronouns in different cases:

    Mick   gave   David   Molly's   towel.
    subject   *indirect*   *possessive*   *object*
                                       object   *noun*

    nominative   *dative*   *genitive*   *accusative*

When Grandpa died   he   left   me   his   mother's gold   watch
       subject   *subject*   *indirect* *possessive* *possessive*   *object*
                                        object   *pronoun*   *noun*

     nominative   *nominative*   *dative*   *genitive*   *genitive*   *accusative*

Case

Mick	(you) throw	me	Molly's	sandshoes	too, please.
the one addressed		indirect object	possessive noun	object	
vocative		dative	genitive	accusative	

Note: All sentences must have a subject; in the above sentence the subject is you (throw). You is understood because it is the same person who is being addressed — in this case Mick.

If you can recognise the case of nouns and pronouns it will help you to understand parts of speech. Remember it is the *work* that a word does in its clause which gives it its part of speech.

Look at the following sentences:

The **motor** needs a clean.
Noun Subject
Nominative Case

I may have to buy a new **motor**
Noun Object
Accusative Case

We have given the **motor** an overhaul.
Indirect Object
Dative Case

Here is a can of **motor** oil.
Adjective qualifying the noun oil
(no case)

Let's **motor** before it gets dark.
Verb
(no case)

Case

A sentence can contain nouns or pronouns in more than one case:

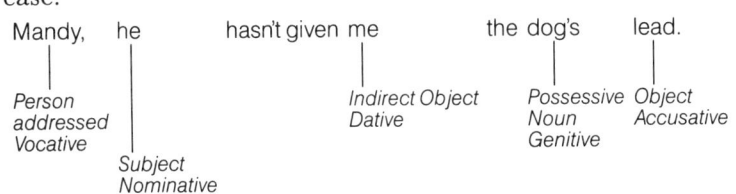

Mandy, — Person addressed, Vocative
he — Subject, Nominative
hasn't given
me — Indirect Object, Dative
the dog's — Possessive Noun, Genitive
lead. — Object, Accusative

Mother. — Vocative
don't give
me — Indirect Object, Dative
any more
medicine. — Object, Accusative

28
Phrases

As we have learnt, a phrase is a group of words without a finite verb. A phrase can do the work of an adjective, an adverb or a noun.

ADJECTIVAL PHRASES

An adjectival phrase tells you more about a noun or a pronoun.

>**Full of smiles** she swept onto the stage.
>Dogs **without collars** will be impounded.
>I love clowns **on a stick**.
>We chose the cake **covered with icing**.
>Take a glass **filled with water**.

ADVERBIAL PHRASES

Adverbial phrases modify the *action of the verb*. They tell when, where, how or why.

Adverbial phrases of time (When):
>Please call me **at seven o'clock**.

During the night a loud bang woke me up.
We shall be rehearsing **all next week**.
He milks the cows **before dawn**.

Adverbial phrases of place (Where):
We sang songs **in the bus**.
The boats were moored **all along the river**.
They had a picnic **beside the lake**.
She pushed her wheelbarrow **through streets broad and narrow**.

Adverbial phrases of manner (How):
He wiped the dipstick **with his handkerchief**.
Dad was singing **at the top of his voice**.
The soldiers advanced **in single file**.
The burglas spoke **in a whisper**.

Adverbial phrases of reason (Why):
She is collecting **for the Blue Nurses**.
David joined in **just for fun**.
They fought to **win the war**.
The rebels captured her **as a hostage**.

NOUN PHRASES

A noun phrase does the work of a single noun. It therefore forms the subject or object of the sentence.

Noun phrase as subject:
Learning Chinese is very hard.
Cruising down the Murray makes a great adventure.

Noun phrase as object:
>I dislike **taking medicine**.
>Hippopotamuses love **rolling in the mud**.

If you can replace the phrase by the word something then it is doing the work of a noun.
>**Something** is very hard.
>**Something** makes a great adventure.
>I dislike **something**.
>Hippopotamuses love **something**.

| In summer, *adverbial phrase of time* | lying under a tree *noun phrase* | thick with branches *adjectival phrase qualifying 'tree'* | is pleasant. |

29
Clauses

Subordinate clauses tell you more about something in the main clause of the same sentence.

Subordinate clauses do the work of adjectives, adverbs or nouns.

You can usually recognise that they are dependent on the main clause because they are joined on to it by a link word. The link word can be a relative pronoun (who, which, etc.) or a conjunction (when, because, etc.).

A subordinate clause can also be dependent on a word in another subordinate clause.

Note: If the conjunction acts purely as a link word to two independent statements of equal weight, then it is not part of the clause.

> Rita ate her chocolate (and) I had a banana.

When the conjunction takes on the function of another part of speech, then it also must be part of the clause.

> Rita ate her chocolate **before** I had my banana.

In the above sentence, before carries meaning connected with time and is therefore an important part of the clause. It is sometimes called an adverbial conjunction.

Rita ate her chocolate **which** had started to melt.

In this sentence, the *link* word is which but this is not a conjunction. It is a relative pronoun in the nominative case being the subject of the verb had and linking it to the word chocolate in the principal clause. Which, therefore, should be included in the clause.

ADJECTIVAL CLAUSES

These clauses, just like simple adjectives, tell you more about a noun. Remember to look for the finite verb.

The old man **who sat next to you on the bus** is my uncle.
Finite verbs: sat, is
Main clause: The old man is my uncle
Link word: who (relative pronoun relating the adjectival clause to the noun **man**)
Adjectival clause: who sat next to you on the bus

This clause *qualifies the noun* man in the main clause.

Dr Barnardo set up a home for children **who were orphans**.
Finite verbs: set up, were
Main clause: Dr Barnardo set up a home for children
Link word: who (relative pronoun relating the adjectival clause to the noun **children**)
Adjectival clause: who were orphans

This clause *qualifies* the noun children in the main clause.

We **took** the chair **that fell apart** to the dump.
Finite verbs: took, fell
Main clause: We took the chair to the dump
Link word: that (relative pronoun)
Adjectival clause: that fell apart

This clause *qualifies* the noun chair in the main clause.

Here comes the reckless driver **who owns the car that rolled over the embankment.**

Finite verbs: comes, owns, rolled.
Main clause: Here comes the reckless driver
Link word 1: who
Subordinate clauses:
1. Adjectival clause: who owns the car

This clause *qualifies* the noun driver in the main clause.

Link word 2: that
2. Adjectival clause: that rolled over the embankment

This clause *qualifies* the noun car in the subordinate clause.

ADVERBIAL CLAUSES

These clauses tell you more about the action of the *verb*. We say that they modify the verb. They usually explain when, where, how or why something happens.

ADVERBIAL CLAUSE OF TIME

This tells you something about the time that a thing happens.

When Father comes home, we'll all have dinner.
|
(At the time that)

Finite verbs: comes, have
Main clause: we'll all have dinner
Link word: when
Subordinate clause: when Father comes home

Adverbial clause of time modifying the verb **have** in main clause.

Link words for adverbial clauses of time are: when, after, until, before, while, during, etc.

You can go swimming **after you have done your homework**.
He played the piano **until all of the guests had arrived**.
Knock **before you go in**.

ADVERBIAL CLAUSE OF PLACE

This clause tells you more about where the actions happens.

Let's put up a sign **where the buses stop**
(at the place that...)

Finite verbs:	Let('s) put, stop
Main clause:	Let('s) put up a sign
Link word:	where
Subordinate clause:	where the buses stop

Adverbial clause of reason, modifying the verb let... put in main clause.

Link words for adverbial clauses of place are: where, wherever.

Koalas live **where eucalyptus trees grow**.
The dog leaves paw marks **wherever he goes**.
Where the bees sucks, there suck I.

ADVERBIAL CLAUSE OF REASON

This clause tells you more about the reason why something happened.

Jeff tripped over **because his shoelace was undone**.
(for the reason that...)

Finite verbs:	tripped, was
Main clause:	Jeff tripped over

Link word:	because
Subordinate clause:	because his shoelace was undone

Adverbial clause of reason modifying the verb tripped in main clause.

Link words for adverbial clauses of reason are: because, for, as, since (meaning because).

>She could not buy the dress **as she had no money**.
>**Since the water is polluted** we shall have to get some elsewehere.
>They wore overcoats, **for it was freezing cold**.
>**Because the creek was up**, we could not get across.

ADVERBIAL CLAUSE OF CONDITION

This clause tells you that in certain circumstances something will happen.

>**If you stack the boxes too high** they will all fall down.
>|
>(on condition that . . .)

Finite verbs:	stack, will fall
Main clause:	they will all fall down
Link word:	if
Subordinate clause:	if you stack the boxes too high

Adverbial clause of condition modifying the verb will fall in the main clause.

Link words for adverbial clauses of condition are: if, whether, unless (negative).

>*If* **you save up enough money** you can pay for the course.
>|
>(on the condition that, in the circumstance that)
>**Unless you have a licence** I cannot employ you.
>|
>(on condition that [not])
>The show must go on **whether there's a power cut or not**.
>　　　　　　　　　　　　　　　|
>　　　　　　　　　　　(in the circumstance that)

ADVERBIAL CLAUSE OF PURPOSE

These clauses tell you the purpose for which something is done.

Aunt Hazel knitted all day **so that the shawl would be finished.**
(in order that)

Finite verbs:	knitted, finished
Main clause:	Aunt Hazel knitted all day
Link words:	so that
Subordinate clause:	so that the shawl would be finished

Adverbial clause of purpose modifying the verb knitted in the main clause.

Link words for adverbial clauses of purpose are: so that, lest (negative i.e. so that . . . not), in order.

The thieves whispered **so that they would not disturb anyone**.
The army climbed the hill **in order to see the enemy advancing**.
Be with us yet, **lest we forget**.

ADVERBIAL CLAUSE OF RESULT

This clause tells you the result of something done.

She danced so beautifully **that the audience clapped for an encore.**
(as a result)

Finite verbs:	danced, clapped
Main clause:	She danced so beautifully
Link word:	that
Subordinate clause:	that the audience clapped for an encore.

Adverbial clause of result modifying the verb danced in the main clause.

Link words for adverbial clauses of result are: so . . . that, such . . . that.

    The crowd was **so** unruly **that the police were called**.
    The old man was **so** angry **that he shook**.
    It was **such** a clear night **that you could count the stars**.

ADVERBIAL CLAUSE OF CONCESSION

This clause tells you that a thing happens in spite of something else.

    Although he had blisters he kept on running.
        |
    (in spite of the fact that)

Finite verbs:	had, kept running
Main clause:	he kept on running
Link word:	although
Subordinate clause:	although he had blisters

Adverbial clause of concession modifying the verb kept running in the main clause.

Link words for adverbial clauses of concession are: although, though, even though, even if, ever, however.

    They played the anthem **although everyone had gone**.
    However much you plead, I shall not give in.
    Even though he is a good actor the film was a flop.

ADVERBIAL CLAUSE OF DEGREE OR COMPARISON

This clause tells you to what degree or in what way something compares with something else. It often contains part of the verb to be.

    The headmaster was **as** cross **as I have ever seen him**.
                    | |
                  (to the extent that)

Finite verbs:	was, have seen
Main clause:	The headmaster was (as) cross
Link word:	as . . . as
Subordinate clause:	as I have ever seen him

Adverbial clause of comparison modifying the verb was in the main clause.

Link words for adverbial clauses of degree are: as much as, just as, than.

> I am **as** fit **as a fiddle** (is).
> She lay **as** still **as she could** (lay).
> The policeman was **as** helpful **as he could be**.

As you see from these examples, in clauses of degree sometimes the verb is omitted.

ADVERBIAL CLAUSE OF COMPARISON

This clause includes a reference to a definite alternative and is introduced by than.

> Eddie is much taller than I am.

Finite verbs:	is, am
Main clause:	Eddie is much taller
Link word:	than
Subordinate clause:	than I am (tall)

Adverbial clause of comparison modifying the verb is in the main clause.

Note: This clause of comparison also often contains part of the verb 'to be'.

The link word for adverbial clauses of degree is: than.

The tortoise will get there sooner **than the hare** (will get there).
I'd rather have a happy home **than (have) all the tea in China**.
Stewart spoke better **than all the other members** (spoke).
I can do anything better **than you** (can).

By substituting one of the short phrases indicated below, you can determine which type of adverbial clause is being used:

Time:	at the time that
Place:	at the place that
Manner:	in such a way that
Reason:	for the reason that
Condition:	on the condition that
Purpose:	in order to
Result:	as a result
Concession:	in spite of the fact that
Degree:	to the extent that
Comparison:	**than** is always the link

Note: The link word can be *misleading*. It is not always a guide to the kind of clause. The same link can introduce several kinds of clause. Therefore it is most important to decide *what part the clause plays in the sentence* — what is it telling you more about?

As can link any of the following adverbial clauses:

an adverbial clause of time:
We strolled **as the sun went down**.

an adverbial clause of reason:
As her shoes were too tight she went barefoot.

an adverbial clause of comparison or degree:
The thief ran **as fast as he could**.

an adverbial clause of manner:
She combed her long hair **as a mermaid does**.

NOUN CLAUSES

A noun clause does the work of a single noun and therefore forms the subject or object of a sentence. If the word something can sensibly replace the clause then it is probably a noun clause.

NOUN CLAUSE AS SUBJECT

>**What I do in my spare time** is my business.
>**Who killed the princess in the tower** is still a mystery.

NOUN CLAUSE AS OBJECT

>We know **that there are millions of stars in the sky**.
>Bob asked Jason **where he had put all the marbles**.

Note: Sometimes noun clauses look like adverbial clauses because they have the same link words. We have to test them to make sure what they do in the sentence.
>I know **where you hid my pencil**.

Does it make sense if we replace the whole clause with the word something?
>I know **something**.

Yes, it does make sense and something (or where you hid my pencil) is the *object* of the verb know in the main clause.

Where can link an adjectival, and adverbial or a noun clause. In an adjectival clause it qualifies a **noun**.
>Let's picnic under the tree **where we met**.

In an adverbial clause it modifies a **verb**.
>The girls swam **where the water was deep**.

In a noun clause it forms the subject or object of a sentence.
>**Where he hides his money** is a mystery to me.
>
> |
> *subject*
>
>I know **where he hides his money.**
>
> |
>   *object*

To the boys' horror, the rope, which was old, broke when James put his weight on it.

>To the boys' horror: *noun phrase.*
>the rope broke: *principal clause.*
>which was old: *adjectival clause.*
>when James put his weight on it: *adverbial clause of time.*

30
Sentence analysis

EXAMPLE OF ANALYSIS OF A COMPOUND COMPLEX SENTENCE

Michael's teeth were so bad and they gave him so much trouble that he went to the dentist, who told him that he should have immediate treatment, before his teeth all dropped out.

Finite verbs:	were, gave, went, told, should have, dropped
Main clauses:	
Main clause A:	Michael's teeth were so bad
Link:	and
Main clause B:	they gave him so much trouble
Subordinate clauses:	
Link:	that
Subordinate clause 1:	that he went to the dentist
(Adverbial clause of result modifying the verbs were and gave in main clauses A and B.)	
Link:	who
Subordinate clause 2:	who told him
(Adverbial clause qualifying the noun dentist in clause 1.)	

Sentence analysis

Link:	that
Subordinate clause:	that he should have immediate treatment

(Noun clause, object of the verb told in subordinate clause 2.)

Link:	before
Subordinate clause 4:	before his teeth all dropped out

(Adverbial clause of time modifying the verb have in subordinate clause 3.)

Not all sentences can be analysed so straightforwardly. Some sentences are more complicated in structure so they need more thought to unravel the dependent clauses.

Here is a more tricky example:

Every afternoon, just before Silver Bud went for her daily walk around the lily pond, Sulkpot Ben Nagnag's Special Guards, armed with large knives and long spears, marched round the garden, and at every hundred paces — which the Captain of the Guard counted loudly under his breath — a Guard was left on duty. From *The Land of Green Ginger* by Noel Langley

Finite verbs:	went, marched, counted, was left
Main clauses:	
Main clause A:	Every afternoon, Sulkpot Ben Nagnag's Special Guards, armed with large knives and long spears, marched round the garden
Link:	and
Main clause B:	at every hundred paces a guard was left on duty
Subordinate clauses:	
Link:	just before
Subordinate clause 1:	just before Silver Bud went for her daily walk around the lily pond

(Adverbial clause of time modifying the verb marched in main clause A.)

Link:	which
Subordinate clause 2:	which the Captain of the Guard counted loudly under his breath

(Adjectival clause qualifying the noun paces in main clause B.)

So you can see that analysing a sentence is a logical process; it can even be fun working out the function of each part of the sentence and seeing how all the parts fit into the pattern of the sentence.

Notice how many colourful phrases ('armed with large knives and long spears', 'under his breath') there are in the second example. It is important to recognise such phrases because they have no finite verb.

Exercises – Part Four

CASE

1. Mark the case of each noun or pronoun in the following:
    a. Now many people use calculators.
    b. A French mathematician invented a remarkable calculating machine.
    c. Blaise Pascal's machine was the first digital calculator.
    d. Different calculators can handle different operations.
    e. This is a solar calculator – Dad's has a battery.
    f. Dale, please lend me your calculator – mine needs a new battery.
    g. The memory is a storage place.
    h. You can show your friends this amazing mathematical trick.
    i. I read about it in Dale's calculator book.
    j. Peter, can you show me how to do that trick?

PHRASES
1. ADJECTIVAL PHRASES
Add suitable adjectival phrases to these sentences:

   a. She tripped over the broom.
   b. Let's buy that bouquet.

c. Pass me the dish.

d. The soldier leapt onto the train.

e. I like thick soup.

f. Dogs can get lost.

g. Look for the car.

h. The moth flew out of the flower pot.

i. He lost his balance.

j. Have you got a spanner?

2. ADVERBIAL PHRASES
Add suitable adverbial phrases to these sentences:

a. I awoke.

b. He shouted.

c. He chased the figure.

d. I ran to the telephone.

e. He hid.

f. They hurried to the vehicle.

g. The car sped away.

h. He tried to read the numberplate.

i. The silence was broken.

j. The police arrived.

3. NOUN PHRASES
Complete the sentences!

a. Elephants enjoy . . . .

b. Mum loves . . . .

c. . . . . makes you tired.

d. .... earns me lots of money.

   e. .... is exciting.

   f. .... brings back memories.

   g. My favourite job is ....

   h. We hoped ....

   i. The boys began ....

   j. .... was all that he wanted.

4. a. Pick out the phrases from the following passage

   We wrapped the stiffening rope round our hands, and drew the sledge up the tracks. There was ice in the air and sharp daggers of cold came stabbing from the edge of night. Frozen darkness lay in the dense woods, only we on our exposed slope were irradiated with the afternoon glow. Then down we went for the last time, and when we sledged in the twilight we felt a wild exhilaration in our veins, we were caught in a web of ice magic. Green swept the west, the crimson clouds turned indigo and darkened to black. Behind us the woods mounted to a blueness which had dropped from the sky over the snow, shadowing it. *Magic In My Pocket*, Alison Uttley (Penguin, 1957)

   b. Name the type of phrase.

CLAUSES

ADJECTIVAL CLAUSES

1. Add adjectival clauses to the following sentences:

   a. The lady sat on the bench.

   b. He asked if I had seen a dog.

   c. He carried a large torch.

   d. A light shone from the window.

   e. They looked at the sky.

ADVERBIAL CLAUSES

2. Add adverbial clauses of different types to each of these sentences. Name the type of clause you have added in each case.

a. Let's stop for lunch.

b. They laughed all the way.

c. Cliff nearly lost his balance.

d. Ben kept waving the flag.

e. They cleared up the mess.

3. Name the kind of adverbial clauses used in these sentences:

   a. If you save up enough money, you can buy a ticket for the match.

   b. After the game is over, we can go to the Pizza Hut.

   c. They rolled the pitch so that it would be in perfect condition.

   d. The crowd cheered as the team ran onto the field.

   e. Garry kicked the ball as far as he could.

   f. Although it was raining, the match continued.

   g. The ball was so slippery that he lost it in the tackle.

   h. He slipped where the pitch was muddy.

   i. He played as if his life depended on it.

   j. They had a party to celebrate because they had won the shield.

NOUN CLAUSES

4. Complete these sentences with a noun clause:

   a. I wish . . . .

   b. . . . . is the subject of my book.

   c. He will tell you . . . .

   d. . . . . I cannot remember.

   e. Do you know . . . . ?

   f. The leader told the boys . . . .

   g. . . . . is written in the manual.

   h. The leader of the expedition planned . . . .

Exercises – Part Four 137

    i.   Please inform the police . . . .

    j.   . . . . is a secret.

5. Pick out the clauses in this passage. Name the type of each one.

> All day we sledged with the brief interval of staggering, snow caked, home for dinner, when we recounted our falls, our triumphs, our express speed. We stayed out till dusk came down from the woods, and the lamplight shone from the house. The western sky glowed golden, the clouds were painted crimson, and the heavenly windows between the thin clouds were of such a radiance we felt God must be there watching through a gap with His angels by His side. Our hearts were filled with bliss. We wanted the day to go on for ever. The sun set in a crack in the hills, and when we flew on scarlet wings we seemed to go towards that golden ball. We walked backward up the hill, lest we should miss a moment of the lovely frosty pageant which stretched like a banner in the west, and we thought we were the only people on earth who saw it. Never a house but our own was in sight, only fields and woods rising from the river to that splendid sky which was our own possession. *Magic In My Pocket* by Alison Uttley (Penguin, 1957)

SENTENCE ANALYSIS

1. Try analysing these sentences.

   a. Every weekend, if he was not needed in the shop, Robbie would slip away to the forest hideaway where his friend, Dave, lived.

   b. Although there were two generations between them, they were great mates who shared many a secret as they sat beside the campfire in the cool evenings.

   c. When the heavy mist came down over the valley, old Dave hung up the storm lantern so that any lost wanderer might see that shelter was handy.

   d. In later years, when Robbie was a grown man, he never forgot what old Dave had told him about the bush which had been his home for so long.

   e. He often thought that he would like to be a hermit too, so that he could live like Dave, away from the city which often seemed so uncaring of the inhabitants who made it.

Part Five
Get it right

31 Some common mistakes explained

32 Knowing the difference!

31
Some common mistakes explained

Once you have learnt how sentences are formed and you can recognise the parts of speech, then it is easy to understand why some ways of saying things are incorrect.

When you know the correct way you will enjoy using it.

I DONE/I SEEN

Done and seen are Past Participles (see p. 25) and therefore need the support of an auxiliary (helping) verb such as have or was to make a tense.

>I **have done** my homework.
>
>My homework **was done**.
>
>They **have seen** the film.
>
>They **were seen** on Friday.

The simple past tense is:
>I **did** my homework.
>
>They **saw** the film.

YOU AND ME

You can be a subject or object of a sentence, but me can be

only the object. Therefore, if the people are the subject of the sentence, I must be used instead of me,
> **You and I** will get top marks.

But, if the people are the object of the sentence, then me is correct.
> Dad will take **you and me** to the show.
> I gave her a present from **you and me**.

WHO OR WHOM?

Who is used for the *subject* of a sentence, whom is used for the *object*. Decide whether you are using the pronoun as the subject or object of your sentence or clause.

Who as subject

> **Who** is that?
> Subject Finite verb

> I know **who** that is.
> That is the man **who** took your ticket.

Whom as object

> **Whom** did you see?
> Object Finite verb

> He told me **whom** you saw.
>   Object

> That is the man **whom** you saw.

Whom as object of a preposition

> For **whom** is this book?
>   Preposition

> With **whom** did you go?
> She told me by **whom** it was written.

Many people drop the use of whom in speech. In written work it is important to use it correctly. Use it whenever it forms the object of a verb or preposition as in the examples shown.

DIFFERENT FROM

Recently different to has become so common that many people do not realise that it is not correct.

Differ means to go in different directions or apart. How can one thing 'go apart *to*' something? or 'go in another direction *to*' a thing? It is a contradiction and therefore cannot be good English.

Different than is also sometimes used. Than is used as a conjunction to introduce the second part of a comparison.

> This tree is taller **than** that one.

In comparison two or more things have a quality in common e.g. tallness. When we say one thing is different from another, we are talking about, what they do *not* have in common!

To be correct, then, we must use different from.

> His present is **different from** yours.
> Manx cats are **different from** the other breeds.
> These biscuits are **different from** the last lot I brought.

DOUBLE NEGATIVES

Sometimes double negatives are used as if for emphasis or just incorrectly.

Just as in Maths — two minuses make a plus — so in language two negatives outweigh each other:

He did**n't** have **no** job, means
He did have a job!

I have**n't** got **no** money, means
I have got some money!

One negative gives the sense required, so correctly we should say:

       He had **no** job.
       He did **not** have a job.
or   He had **not** got a job.
and I have **no** money.
       I do **not** have any money.
       I have **not** got any money.

Hardly is also a partial negative meaning 'not easily', or 'not much'. It is therefore the same as having *two* negatives to say It didn't hardly rain.

Correctly, we should say:
       It hardly rained.
i.e. It (not much) rained.

and He wouldn't hardly speak to me

should be correctly   He would hardly speak to me.

TWO COMPARATIVES/SUPERLATIVES

More is a comparative. It is incorrect to use two comparatives together, so we cannot say:
       This one is **more lovelier**

Some common mistakes explained

Instead we say:
>This one is **more** lovely.
>
>or   This one is **lovelier**.

Similarly we cannot say more better or more worse. Thus instead of:
>This child is **more** good.

We say:
>This child is **better**.
>
>That one is **bad**.
>
>But this one is **worse**.

Similarly we cannot have two superlatives such as most stupidest, most prettiest. We say:
>He was the most **stupid** boy.
>
>or   He was the **stupidest** boy.
>
>They have the most **pretty** garden.
>
>or   They have the **prettiest** garden.

Note: Perfect, excellent, unique are superlative forms, so they cannot be used with more or most.
>Unique means one of a kind.

Thus:
>This is the only one that has ever been found. It is unique.

One cannot compare anything of which there is only one!

Nothing can be better than perfect and nothing can excel excellence, so it is also wrong to modify such words with very, rather, etc.

Thus; we must not say he made a most perfect landing or that she gave a very excellent performance.
>but, He made a **perfect** landing.
>
>She gave an **excellent** performance.

LIKE/AS THOUGH

It is becoming a common mistake to use like in the place of as though or as if.

Like can form a preposition meaning 'in the manner of'. In this case it is followed by an object, usually a noun, noun phrase or noun clause:

>He sings like a bird (sings).
>We think like politicians.
>He ran like a hunted deer.

BUT, If we are using an adverbial clause of condition (see p. 123), we must use the correct link, as though or as if.

>Now fall down **as if** you are dying.
>He whispered **as though** he were afraid.

We can say:
>He sang *like* **a bird.**
> |
>   *noun*

(ie as melodically, beautifully, tonefully, naturally as a bird.)

but He sang ***as though*** **he were a bird.**
                      |
                adverbial clause
                of condition

(ie in imitation of a bird, pretending to be a bird.)

32
Know the difference!
Words that are often misused

Once you know the eight parts of speech and how they are used it is easy to understand how to use the following words correctly.

AFFECT/EFFECT

Affect is a verb meaning 'to influence'.
Effect is a noun meaning 'result'.
Thus something affects you and produces the effect.
> How did the accident **affect** your brother?
> The accident had a bad **effect** on him.

Effect can also be a verb meaning 'bring about'.
> The new signs **effected** an improvement in road conditions.

**ALLUDE/ELUDE
(ALLUSION, ELUSION, ILLUSION)**

These words are both verbs, but they have quite different meanings.

If you allude to something you refer to it indirectly, hence allusion means 'an indirect reference'.
> He said nothing about their quarrel, but he made an **allusion** to the strain in their relationship.

Elude means 'escape by skilful means'; hence elusion means 'a skilful escape'.

> He **eluded** the police for five hours.
> The public blamed the **elusion** of the prisoner on the lack of trained policemen.

Illusion means 'a false perception of the senses'.

> optical **illusion**.
> A mirage is an optical **illusion** often seen in the desert.

It is not related to a verb in English.

ALL READY/ALREADY

All ready is correct when ready is an adjective qualifying all.

> We are **all ready** to start.
> Are the letters **all ready** to post?

Already is an adverb.

> I have finished my homework **already**.
> It is **already** time for bed.

ALL RIGHT/ALRIGHT

All right is correct when right is an adjective qualifying all.

> Your sums are **all right**. (i.e. **all correct**)
> We were **all right** not to go. (i.e. **a proper decision was made**)

ALRIGHT

By analogy (using it similarly) with already, alright is now acceptable in certain cases:

1. As an adverb:
   > If you feel **alright** you may go to the races. (i.e. **well enough**)

2. As a reply meaning assent:
    'Please get the washing in.'
    'Alright.' (i.e. **O.K, sure**)

AMOUNT/NUMBER

Amount is used for a quantity that cannot be numbered.
    some sand — an **amount** of sand.
    We have an **amount** of liquid.

Number is used for things that can be counted.
    A **number** of books is missing.
    We have a **number** of tools for sale.

Note also: fewer deals with *number.*
    He had **fewer** toffees than I did.

and less deals with *amount.*
    Mother ordered **less** milk this morning.

ANTE/ANTI

These are two prefixes with quite different meanings.

Ante (from Latin) means 'before'.
    antenatal — before birth.
    antediluvian — before the flood, or antiquated.

Anti (from Greek) means 'against'.
    antibody — substance in the blood reacting against poison or bacteria.
    antisocial — against being social.

ANY WAY/ANYWAY

Any way is correct when any is an adjective qualifying way.
> There isn't **any way** of doing that.
> He did not know of **any way** to go.

Anyway is an adverb meaning 'in any case'.
> We are not going **anyway**.
> **Anyway**, I didn't want to go.

BETWEEN/AMONG

Between is used for separating *two things*.
> **Between** you and me, that was a fake.
> This is to be divided **between** Billy and Tom.

Among is used for separating *more than two things*.
> Billy and Tom may share it **among** their friends.

BESIDE/BESIDES

Besides means 'at the side of'.
> They camped **beside** the river.

and in the expression
> We were **beside** ourselves with fear.

Besides means 'in addition, moreover'.
> He had to pay the taxi **besides** the rent.
> I was too sick to go. **Besides**, I had not been invited.

BORROW/LEND

You borrow if you take something temporarily from someone else. You cannot lend from someone, nor can you have a lend because lend is not a noun.
> Please may I **borrow** your bicycle?

Know the difference!

If you lend something you allow someone to take it temporarily from you.

>Yes, I shall **lend** you my bicycle.

Thus: The one who gives, lends.
      The one who receives, borrows.

BURST/BUST

Burst is a verb meaning 'to break open or explode'.

>Take care the bag does not **burst**.
>
>The pipe **burst** when it froze.

Bust and busted are slang.

CAN/MAY

Can is a *principal transitive* verb (not an auxiliary) meaning able to or permitted to.

>He **can** yodel.
>*verb infinitive*
>*object*

May is an *auxiliary* verb which expresses uncertainty.

>It **may** freeze tonight.
>*auxiliary verb*

May can also express permission but still as an auxiliary verb.

>You **may** lead the band.
>*auxiliary verb*

May rather than can to express permission appears to have been a matter of polite fashion, rather than accurate usage. This discrimination is currently losing support.

CENSOR/CENSURE

Censor is a verb or noun.
As a *verb* it means 'to suppress or restrict publication'.
> The board **censors** all blue films.

The *noun* is the person who censors.
> The **censor** banned the film.

Censure is a verb meaning 'to find fault with, or reprove'.
> The boys were **censured** for their bad behaviour at the football match.

COMPLEMENT/COMPLIMENT

When learning these words, to remember which is which it is a good idea to stress the pronunciation of the middle vowel, thus relating each to its source.

Complement means 'that which completes'.
> The strong black coffee was a perfect **complement** to the delicious meal.

It can also be used as a verb:
> The autumn flowers **complemented** the warm colours of the room.

Compliment is a polite expression of praise.
> He paid me a **compliment** on my dress.
> Thank you for the **compliment**.

or as a verb:
> He **complimented** me on my dress.

COMPRISE/INCLUDE

Comprise is used when *all* the components are mentioned.

> The house **comprises** nine rooms.
>
> All the actors who **comprise** the cast of *Hello Dolly* were invited to the dinner.

Include is used when we refer to *only one* or *some* of the components.

> I hope they **include** Simon O'Donnell in the team.
>
> Please **include** your own comments in your answer.

CONTINUAL/CONTINUOUS

Continual is an adjective describing something which keeps happening, that is, it is frequent, but interrupted.

> I have **continual** problems with the plumbing in this house.

Continuous, also an adjective, describes something which goes on without interruption.

> The **continuous** hissing noise from the factory chimney is driving me crazy.

COUNSEL/COUNCIL

Counsel is a noun meaning 'advice'.

> You should take **counsel**.

It can also be used as a verb: to give counsel.

> We **counsel** young married couples.

Hence: counsellor: one who advises; adviser.

Council is a noun meaning an assembly of persons selected for making decisions.

> The **council** debated the matter for six hours.

Hence: councillor: one who serves on a Council.

DISINTERESTED/UNINTERESTED

Disinterested means 'not biased by personal interest'. A disinterested party is one who does not stand to gain by the outcome of a matter.

> They asked him to be the judge because he was **disinterested** in the result.

Uninterested means 'having no concern about something'.

> Jack was **uninterested** in the job he was offered.

ELIGIBLE/ILLEGIBLE

Both these words are adjectives but have different meanings.

Eligible describes something which is suitable to be chosen, or qualified to compete.

> If you were born during 1973 you are **eligible** for this race.
> Is this painting **eligible** for the Exhibition?

Illegible means 'unable to be read'.

> I cannot read it. Your writing is **illegible**.

Legible means 'able to be read'.
   Please write it again, so that it is **legible**.

FARTHER/FURTHER

These words are often mistakenly used as though they were interchangeable.

Farther relates to distance and literally means 'more far'.

> Micky threw the ball **farther** than I did.

Further means 'in addition'.

> We shall have to discuss this matter **further**.

Know the difference!

GOOD/WELL

Good is an *adjective* and therefore tells us more about a noun or pronoun.

    These **cakes** are **good**.

    He is **good** at diving.

    Paul painted a very **good picture**.

Well is an *adverb* and therefore tells us more about a verb, that is, about *how* something is done.

    Mike **performed well** in the championships.

    The boys **cooked** really **well** at the camp.

Thus, we must not say

    I think I did **good** in the exam.

but

    I think I did **well** in the exam.
    I wrote a really **good** essay.
    I think I wrote it **well**.

HISTORICAL/HISTORIC

Historical is an adjective describing something belonging to the past.

    These **historical** documents must be preserved carefully.

Historic refers to something of particular significance in history.

    The opening of the new Parliament House was a **historic** event.

IF/WHETHER

If is the conjunction which introduces an adverbial clause of condition.

> He puts his fingers in his ears **if** I song.

But where the two alternatives are stated, whether is preferable.

> I shall go **whether** you come or not.

Whether must be used to introduce a noun clause.

> I asked him **whether** I should sing.

INCREDIBLE/INCREDULOUS

Incredible means 'could not be believed'. It describes a happening or something told, such as a story or an excuse.

> The treasurer's figures on the balance of payment were **incredible**.

Incredulous describes a person who does not believe something.

> He was **incredulous** when he heard the treasurer's statement.

INVALUABLE

Invaluable does not mean 'not valuable', but of so much worth that it is 'unable to be valued'.

> Their help during the floods was **invaluable**.

LEAVE/LET

These words do not mean the same thing.
Leave means 'depart or cause to remain'.

Know the difference!

Let means 'allow'.
> We can say, 'Leave me alone' 'or permit'. (ie cause me to remain alone; depart without me.)
> Or we can say, 'Let me go'. (ie allow/permit me to go.)

LIABLE/LIBEL

Liable is an adjective meaning either 'open' or 'under obligation'.
> His accounts are **liable** to be checked by the Income Tax Department.
> A man is **liable** to pay his debts.

Libel is either a verb or a noun meaning 'slander'.
> The newspaper has **libelled** you.
> You should sue the newspaper for **libel**.

LIE/LAY

Lie is an intransitive verb meaning 'to be in a horizontal position'.
> **Lie** down!

Lay is a transitive verb, which means that it must take an *object*:
> Please **lay** the **table.**
> |
>   *object*

> Chickens **lay eggs**.
> |
>   *object*

The forms of these two verbs are not the same.

Present	Past	Present participle	Past participle
lie (down)	lay	lying	lain
lay (an egg)	laid	laying	laid

METER/METRE

A meter is an instrument for measuring, hence:
  gas-o-meter for measuring gas.
  term-o-meter for measuring temperature.

Note: in pronunciation the stress is on the syllable preceding the meter.

A metre is a unit of measurement.
  You will require eight metres of cloth for your curtains.

Hence also: kilometre, centimetre, millimetre.

Note: The stress in this case is on the first syllable.

Metre also describes any regular pattern of poetic rhythm.

PRACTICE/PRACTISE

Practice is the noun, practise the verb.
  A good tip for remembering is that ice is a noun.

noun	verb
advice	advise
device	devise

However, these two are easier to remember as the two forms are pronounced differently.

PRINCIPAL/PRINCIPLE

Principal is an noun or adjective meaning 'first in rank'.
> Please take this letter to the Principal.
> Wool is the principal export of Australia.

Principle is a noun meaning 'fundamental truth, law of nature, or personal code of conduct'.
> This machine works on the same principle as a steam engine.
> I refused on principle to take money for the job.

PROTAGONIST

This word is often used as if it were the opposite of antagonist. The first syllable, pro, comes from Greek and means 'first'. A protagonist is the chief actor in a play, leader of a campaign or movement.
> Emily Pankhurst was a protagonist of the Suffragettes.

REASON

The reason is that is the correct expression.
> The reason for my being late **is that** my car broke down.

That my car broke down is the complement of the verb is, and is therefore a noun clause.

It is incorrect to say the reason is because as because introduces an adverbial clause of reason and *cannot* introduce a noun clause.

It is also repetitious to say 'The reason why . . .'

A correct sentence would be:
> The reason that I failed was tiredness.

or   The reason for my failure was tiredness.

STATIONARY/STATIONERY

Stationary is an adjective describing the state of remaining in one place, that is, not moving.

> Children must not board the bus until it is stationary.

Stationery is a collective noun meaning 'writing materials'.

> We supply textbooks, but students must bring their own stationery.

Note: Tips for remembering: station*a*ry — st*a*nd
station*e*ry — p*e*n

TEACH/LEARN

As with borrow and lend these two words are not interchangeable.

The one who gives instruction teaches. The one who receives instructions learns.

You can teach somebody but you cannot 'learn' anyone. We learn from our teachers.

> Let me **teach** you how to play your guitar.
> Thank you; I should like to **learn** how to play it.

THAT/WHICH/WHO(M)

These are relative pronouns which introduce an adjectival clause and therefore form the subject or object of that clause.
Who refers to people.
Which refers to things.
That may refer to either.

> There is the man **who/that** slipped on the banana skin.
> There is the banana skin **which/that** he slipped on.

Whom can only be the object.

> The boy **whom/that** we saw in the shop dropped the banana skin.

THEM/THOSE

See the section on Pronouns Part I (especially p. ?? and p. ??) for the information about the use of these words.

Them is a pronoun which means that it stands in the place of a noun. Therefore we cannot include the noun *as well as* the pronoun.

It is therefore wrong to say:
> We saw them trucks by the road.

We therefore say:
> We saw **them** by the road.
> |
>   pronoun

Or if we wish to point out which particular trucks we are speaking about:
> We saw **those**   trucks by the road.
> | |
>   adjective noun

N.B. Those can also be a pronoun when it stands in place of a noun:
> We saw **those**   by the road.
> |
>   pronoun

> Hang **those**   up in your cupboard.
> |
>   pronoun

Them is never an adjective.

TRY TO

It is preferable to say try to rather than try and, because the trying is involved in the action in question.
> **Try to be** earlier next time.

The trying and the action are not two separate things as 'try and be earlier' suggests.

Exercises — Part Five

SOME COMMON MISTAKES EXPLAINED

Write in the correct word/s.

1. **DONE/SEEN**
    a. This morning I . . . . a lot of work. did/done
    b. Yesterday we . . . . Phantom of the Opera on T.V. saw/see
    c. I know what you . . . . just now. done/did
    d. We . . . . the Railway Museum. have seen/seen
    e. I hope they . . . . the repairs on my car today. done/did

2. **I/ME**
    a. I hope he will take you and . . . . to the circus.
    b. Tomorrow you and . . . . should get our exam results.
    c. Goodnight to you all from Jerry and . . . .
    d. It seems strange to you and . . . . but it's true.
    e. He came while you and . . . . were out.

3. **WHO/WHOM**
    a. . . . . pushed that boy into the swimming pool.
    b. . . . . did you tell?

c. I can guess .... did it.

   d. Do you know .... he pushed in?

   e. By .... was he pulled out?

4. **DIFFERENT FROM/THAN/TO**
   a. I am darker than Brad and his hair is different .... mine. from/than

   b. This method is different .... the one you use. to/from

   c. I do it differently .... you. from/to

5. **DOUBLE NEGATIVES**
Write correctly in two different ways.

   a. That dog doesn't have no tail.

   b. My father hasn't hardly got any hair.

   c. He can't hardly kick any goals these days.

   d. I hadn't never seen my Grandpa before.

6. **COMPARISON**
Insert the correct word

   a. Which is the (high) of those two church spires.

   b. This is the (old) church in the city.

   c. Which has the (tall) steeple, this one or St. Pauls.

   d. Jack goes to church (often) than I do.

   e. Murn would like it (good) if we went (much) weeks.

7. **LIKE/AS THOUGH**
   a. Gwen wants a horse .... the one over there.

   b. Her people spend money .... it grows on trees.

   c. Her mother always looks .... she has stepped out of Vogue.

   d. Her father drives .... a maniac.

   e. Gwen always feels .... they forget about her.

Exercises – Part Five

KNOW THE DIFFERENCE

Fill in the blanks.
1. **AFFECT/EFFECT**
    a. What . . . . will daylight saving have on your business?
    b. How will it . . . . the farmers?
    c. Dad says it will have a bad . . . . on the dairymen.
    d. It probably won't . . . . us very much.
    e. The . . . . may not be known for some time.

2. **ALLUSION/ELUSION/ILLUSION**
    a. I hope you are not under the . . . . that Neville committed the crime.
    b. The prosecutor made an . . . . to Neville's debts in his submission.
    c. The case was complicated by the . . . . of the chief witness.
    d. He liked to create the . . . . that he was rich.
    e. The defendant is offended by your . . . . to his past.

3. **ALL READY/ALREADY   ALL RIGHT/ALRIGHT**
    a. Are you . . . . to go back to camp?
    b. The bus has come . . . .
    c. The girls are . . . . in it!
    d. Have you got your tickets . . . . to be checked?
    e. Did you find the garage . . . . ?
    f. Is it . . . . to leave now?
    g. Your answers to the questions are . . . .
    h. Some of the girl's were wrong, but the boy's were . . . .

4. **AMOUNT/NUMBER**
Fill in with a suitable article if required:
   a. They reported .... of missing persons.
   b. .... of food was left in the truck.
   c. We took a large .... of tins of meat.
   d. I can't tell you the .... of people at the show.
   e. We need to know the .... of firewood required.

5. **ANTI/ANTE**
   a. Most of us have .... bodies in our blood.
   b. Genealogy can tell us something about our .... cedents.
   c. The delegates passed through the .... room into the main hall.
   d. Milk is a good .... dote to many poisons.
   e. The government introduced new .... smoking laws.

6. **BETWEEN/AMONG**
   a. Share this cake .... the girls.
   b. There is a close relationship .... the members of our family.
   c. The incident caused ill-feeling .... him and me.
   d. We were asked not to sail .... the two buoys.
   e. It is fun to sail .... all the coral outcrops.

7. **BESIDE/BESIDES**
   a. Come and sit .... me.
   b. There were many other students there .... me.
   c. .... I was feeling too sick to attend.
   d. I huddled .... my horse to keep warm.
   e. After losing her bank book she was .... herself with worry.

8. **BORROW/LEND**
   a. He asked us if he could .... my tie.
   b. I was quite happy to .... him it.
   c. If you .... something you should take care to give it back.
   d. Can I .... your umbrella?
   e. Yes, but don't .... it to anyone else.

9. **BURST/BUST**
   a. He cried when his balloon ....
   b. We watched as the bud .... open.
   c. A stone must have .... my radiator.

10. **CENSOR/CENSURE**
    a. I think they should .... him for his rudeness.
    b. I hope they don't .... our letters at the gaol.
    c. The .... will come today.
    d. The boss is going to .... him for interrupting.
    e. Most countries wanted to .... the satanic book.

11. **COMPLIMENT/COMPLEMENT**
    a. Every lady enjoys a ....
    b. The orchid will .... her new dress.
    c. He paid us the ....s of the season.
    d. What shall we drink to .... this wonderful dinner?
    e. Let's .... the cook before we leave.

12. **COMPRISE/INCLUDE**
    a. Let's .... all the teams in the invitation.
    b. Please .... the wine in the bill.
    c. The meal will .... five courses.
    d. Don't .... soup in my order.
    e. This gathering ....s all the clubs in the city.

13. CONTINUAL/CONTINUOUS
a. Gladys gets fed up with her neighbour's .... complaints.

b. The burglar alarm lets out a .... high-pitched sound.

c. This bulb will give .... light all night.

d. Her son's .... spending sprees cause her much worry.

e. Thieves are a .... threat to the peace of the suburb.

14. COUNSEL/COUNCIL/COUNCILLOR/COUNSELLOR
a. The .... sat for four hours, discussing the problem.

b. The .... visited her home to advise her.

c. The chaplain frequently ....s the young recruits.

d. The plans will have to be submitted to the .... for approval.

e. Only three of the elected .... were present.

15. DISINTERESTED/UNINTERESTED
a. I am totally .... in her affairs.

b. They chose me to lead the inquiry as I was a .... party.

c. Juries are made up of a body of .... persons.

d. We are not altogether .... in the outcome.

e. Dad sold the property as his sons were all .... in farming.

16. ELIGIBLE/ILLEGIBLE/LEGIBLE
a. Are you .... for this job?

b. All writing must be ....

c. If your address is .... the letter may not reach its destination.

d. All .... persons may apply.

e. All holders of current cards are .... for discount.

Exercises – Part Five

17. **FARTHER/FURTHER**
    a. You are not to cycle . . . . than the road end.
    b. They are taking the road . . . . and . . . . into the forest.
    c. . . . . to your request, we shall call a meeting.
    d. He refused to discuss this matter any . . . .
    e. Please bury the rubbish . . . . from the camp.

18. **GOOD/WELL**
    a. How . . . . do you think you did in the Eistedfodd?
    b. If she performs . . . . Mother will take us to the finals.
    c. If there is a . . . . audience, she will respond . . . .
    d. You did a . . . . job today, the music was . . . . too.
    e. Your dance was . . . . – you did it . . . .

19. **HISTORICAL/HISTORIC**
    a. We are all happy to be here on this . . . . occasion.
    b. This library contains manuscripts of . . . . interest.
    c. The Battle of Waterloo was truly . . . .
    d. That . . . . building has been destroyed by fire.
    e. These items are of . . . . importance.

20. **IF/WHETHER**
    a. We wondered . . . . the match would be cancelled.
    b. I shall go . . . . it stops raining.
    c. He says we won't know 'til we arrive . . . . it has been cancelled or not.
    d. It will be a pity . . . . we have to come home.
    e. I don't know . . . . I should go or not.

Exercises — Part Five

21. **INCREDIBLE/INCREDULOUS**
    a. His life story is truly . . . .
    b. When I told him about my adventures he was . . . .
    c. He had some . . . . stories to tell.
    d. The size of the beast was . . . .
    e. I was . . . . to start with, but now I realise it was all true.

22. **LIABLE/LIBEL**
    a. Don't trust him — he is . . . . to let you down.
    b. If he tells them you are untrustworthy that is . . . .
    c. You could be charged with . . . . for saying that.
    d. You are . . . . to be charged with . . . .
    e. . . . . is an indictable offence.
    f. The judge is . . . . to convict you.
    g. I think he is . . . . to go to gaol.

23. **LIE/LAY**
Provide the correct form in the spaces:

    a. Gravel had been . . . . all over the road.
    b. The roadmen . . . . the gravel on Friday.
    c. He had . . . . there for some time.
    d. The men found him . . . . there, while they were . . . . the gravel.
    e. He . . . . on the grass by the road.

24. **PRACTISE/PRACTICE**
    a. Eric does his saxophone . . . . every day.
    b. He has to . . . . regularly.
    c. Do you listen to him . . . . ?
    d. . . . . makes perfect.
    e. I would rather . . . . than play football.

Exercises — Part Five

25. **PRINCIPAL/PRINCIPLE**
    a. In a pantomime the .... is always played by someone of the opposite sex.
    b. Our teacher is going to ask the .... if we can put on a pantomime.
    c. I think everyone should take part as a matter of ....
    d. The .... reason for staging pantomimes is to make people laugh.
    e. Usually a moral .... is demonstrated in the story.

26. **METER(S)/METRE(S)**
    a. Telecom installed a unit .... in the motel.
    b. The nearest telephone was five hundred .... away.
    c. A hydro .... can show the density of sugar in a syrup.
    d. What .... did Shakespeare use in his sonnets?
    e. The .... reader visits monthly to measure the amount of electricity we use.

27. **STATIONARY/STATIONERY**
    a. The .... for this office costs a fortune.
    b. When the armed robbers came in, they ordered us to remain ....
    c. They took only money, none of the ....
    d. The get-away car stood .... at the entrance while the thieves were inside.
    e. As the thieves sped away they crashed into a .... truck.

28. **THEM/THOSE**
    a. We gave .... some cakes.
    b. We gave the boys .... cakes.
    c. .... will be good for ....
    d. .... boys like cakes.
    e. We shall take .... to get some more of ....

Part Six

Answers to exercises

Answers to exercises

PART ONE

NOUNS

3. a. regiment, battalion, etc.
   b. congregation
   c. choir
   d. audience
   e. cast
   f. queue
   g. fleet
   h. convoy column

4.
common	proper	collective	proper *(abstract)*
cave	St Paul	traffic	comfort
piecrust	California	team	fear
honey	Easter	tribe	journey
prunes	Prince Edwad	bunch	love
emu			loss
orange			greed
lassie			

SINGULAR AND PLURAL

5.
singular	plural	singular	plural
leg	legs	berry	berries
dish	dishes	weekend	weekends
way	ways	sheep	sheep
leaf	leaves	lunch	lunches
lorry	lorries	icecream	icecreams

6. truck (sing.)   windows (pl.)   office (sing.)
   notes (pl.)   piano (sing.)   staircase (sing.)

7. trucks   offices   pianos
   staircases

8. window   note

175

MASCULINE, FEMININE AND NEUTER
9.

masculine	feminine	neuter
soldier	witch	truck
airman	maid	storm
pig	goose	rubber
stag	mare	apple
youth	princess	horn

PRONOUNS

1.
   a.
pronouns	type
I	personal
it	personal
myself	reflexive

   b. these — demonstrative
   c. she — personal
   d. that — demonstrative; yours — possessive
   e. you — personal; he — personal; us — personal

   f.
pronoun	type
who	interrogative
this	demonstrative
no-one	indefinite

   g. he — personal; each — distributive; it — personal
   h. somebody — indefinite; these — demonstrative
   i. that — demonstrative; who — relative; himself — reflexive
   j. everyone — indefinite; me — personal; it — personal

VERBS
3. a. keys (direct object); me (indirect object)
   b. friends (indirect object); pancakes (direct object)
   c. snake (direct object)
   d. sentence (direct object); objects (direct object)

PARTICIPLES

| collapsed | drunk | dealt | faltered | hidden | felt |
| brought | lost | swept | torn | | |

REGULAR AND IRREGULAR VERBS
8.

regular	irregular
wept	dug
dripped	striven
floated	thrown
lost	
smelt	
lent	
fought	

TENSES
9. a.
are cooking	—	present continuous
will be	—	future
leaves	—	present
were playing	—	past continuous
will ring	—	future

Answers to exercises

c. is snoring — present
will be cooking — future
will be — future
drives — present
tore — past

d. is riding
shall be having
is singing
was feeling
will be planting

COMPLEMENTS

10. a. a clown in the circus — noun phrase
amused — single adjective
a good year for peaches — noun phrase
a handsome prince — noun phrase
our next Prime Minister — noun phrase

c. a striking building
a very public-spirited man
very proud of their hall
a great asset to their social activities

ADJECTIVES

1. a.

noun	adjective
noon	full, bright
ginger	green
trees	ginger
Ginger	sparkling, sugar-coated, Green
flowers	bright, beauteous
grass	soft, velvety
lilies	water
stream	cheerful, little, hubble-bubbling

4. a. cheerful, cheerless, cheery
hopeful, hopeless
fearful, fearsome, fearless
loathsome, loatheful
thankless, thankful
lonesome, lonely
loveless, lovely, lovable
resistible, resistant, irresistible
senseless, sensible, sensuous, sensitive, sensual
meaningful, meaningless

5.

positive	comparative	superlative
ugly	uglier	ugliest
plain	plainer	plainest
dry	drier	driest
complicated	more complicated	most complicated
little	less	least

tiny	tinier	tiniest
bald	balder	baldest
trustworthy	more trustworthy	most trustworthy
funny	funnier	funniest
bad	worse	worst

6. a. older, eldest
   b. more beautiful
   c. most
   d. better (more)
   e. heaviest

ADVERBS
1. a. rudely   b. bitterly   c. wildly   d. feast   e. too

2. a. smartly   lazily
      loudly   loosely
      wisely   prettily
      foolishly   falsely
      well   contentedly

PREPOSITIONS
2. on from in down in of to above of round towards into in across onto in with through behind in without

ARTICLES, CONJUNCTIONS AND INTERJECTIONS
2. a. until (till)   b. because as while
   c. before when if   d. although until because etc.
   e. if   f. although
   g. (in order) to

PARSING
1. a. Phil   proper noun   b. There   adverb
      left   verb   is   verb
      his   possessive adjective   a   article
      dirty   adjective   huge   adjective
      shoes   noun   black   adjective
      at   preposition   spider   noun
      the   article   in   preposition
      door.   noun   your   possessive adjective
                                            desk.   noun

   c. A   article   d. A   article
      family   collective noun   helicopter   noun
      of   preposition   hovered   verb
      ducks   noun   near   preposition
      crossed   verb   my   possessive adjective
      the   article   balcony.   noun
      road   noun
      in front of prepositional phrase
      us.   pronoun

Answers to exercises

e. | The | article
| farmer's | noun
| wife | noun
| cut | verb
| off | adverb
| their | possessive adjective
| tails | noun
| with | preposition
| the | article
| carving | adjective
| knife. | noun

f. | Huge | adjective
| uneven | adjective
| hailstones | noun
| covered | verb
| the | article
| ground. | noun

g. | Craig | noun
| kicked | verb
| the | article
| ball | noun
| straight | adverb
| between | preposition
| the | article
| posts | noun

h. | Suddenly | adverb
| I | pronoun
| was | verb
| was swept | verb
| into | preposition
| the | article
| sea | noun
| by | preposition
| a | article
| giant | adjective
| wave. | noun

i. | I | pronoun
| managed | verb
| to | preposition
| get | verb
| my | possessive adjective
| luggage | collective noun
| onto | preposition
| the | article
| correct | adjective
| flight. | noun

j. | The | article
| superb | adjective
| open | adjective
| scenery | noun
| of | preposition
| the | article
| Ranges | proper noun
| contrasts | verb
| dramatically | adverb
| with | preposition
| the | article
| magnificent | adjective
| world | noun
| within | preposition
| the | article ·
| forests. | noun

KINDS OF SENTENCES

1.   *clause/s*   *sentence type*
   a. (The bus *will come* past at 4.30)   simple
   b. (Firemen *broke in*) . . . (*helped* . . . out)   compound
   c. (He *fed* . . . crumbs)   simple
   d. (We . . . have . . . party) (when . . . *comes*)   complex
   e. (There *came* . . . spider) . . . (*sat down* . . . her)   compound
   f. (Your . . . *will fall* out) (if . . . *forget* . . . them)   complex
   g. (Hannibal *crossed* . . . elephants)   simple

h. (He *opened* . . . door) . . . (*was forced* . . . smoke)   compound
i. (When . . . *hit*) (we *had to* . . . windows)   complex
j. (Several . . . *went past*) . . . (none . . . *saw* us)   compound
   Note: In verbs such as broken in, sat down etc., the adverb may be included as part of the verb.

PART TWO

CAPITAL LETTERS
1. a. In the Christmas holidays we went to Dreamworld, but at Easter we are going to Disneyland in America.
   b. Hayley Lewis won five Gold Medals at the Commonwealth Games.
   c. John Travolta was born on 18 February 1954; do you know when Jason Donovan was born?
   d. Sandy took his new book, *Charlie and The Chocolate Factory* to school to show to Mr Kennedy.
   e. Dad reads the *Daily Sun*, Mum reads her *Women's Weekly*, but I like the comic strips, especially Tom and Jerry.

PUNCTUATION MARKS
1. a. One passenger jumped out just before the plane dived.
   b. Jump! Jump! We are going to crash!
   c. Did you see where the plane landed?
   d. Wow! They are lucky to be alive!
   e. Shaken but unhurt, he scrambled to his feet.
   f. The parachute, which had saved his life, lay limp and torn across the stubble.
   g. Ben, do you ever think you will go flying again?
   h. Of course, Danny, but I have learned from the experience.
   i. Parts of the plane, tail, undercarriage, seat and propeller were strewn all over the paddock.
   j. The plane was a wreck, but, oh boy! you should see Ben's new one — a Cessna 120.

INVERTED COMMAS
1. a. 'Why didn't you come to my party?' asked Des.
   b. 'I had promised to go to Damien's party,' replied Belinda, 'Didn't you get my reply?'
   c. 'No, did you send one?' answered Des, 'I was expecting you to turn up.'
   d. 'Sorry,' answered Belinda, 'I wish I had come to yours instead.'
   e. 'You missed a good night, Belinda,' called Phil, through the window, 'Never mind, come inside and join us.'
   f. Belinda stepped inside followed by Des. 'Whew! It's hot in here,' she cried, 'Can we open some windows?'
   g. 'Yes do,' called Mum from the kitchen, 'I was trying to keep out the insects while I was cooking.'
   h. 'Don't worry,' laughed Des, 'We all like squashed fly cake, don't we girls?'
   i. 'Well if you behave yourselves you can have some of the squashed fly cake,' said Mum, handing out a tray. 'There you are boys and girls.'
   j. 'Oh, Mrs Randall! What a super cake!' burst out Belinda, with her mouth full, 'Would you let me have the recipe?'

Answers to exercises

THE APOSTROPHE
1. a. Linda's pool   b. Nev's   c. Mum's   d. Ken's   e. aunt's
2. a. Julie's   b. sister's   c. Nev's, Nev's
   d. Linda's, Linda's, Mum's   e. Mum's, Uncle Dick's (or Dicks')
3. a. the Jules'   b. Dad's, St Patrick's, Tom's
   c. Sam Jule's, it's, Turner's,   d. Turner's, Sam Jule's
   e. the Jules', Mrs Jule's
4. a. It is a lovely day   b. It has, its trunk
   c. It is a bun, its baby, it is only   d. It is funny, its mother's leg, its trunk
   e. It is hungry, it is looking, its feed
   f. it is feeding time   g. it is getting, its dinner
   h. it is our dinnertime, its meat
   i. its meat, it is better   j. it is better, if it is open it has got, its door
5. a. I am   b. Have not   c. I have
   d. You are   e. He has
6. a. Where've   didn't   b. They're   they've
   c. I'd   can't   d. You're   should've
   d. When'll   I'm

7. She would have liked to have gone to see Starlight Express, but she could not because she had 'flu, so if you will get her a ticket when you are in town, she will be able to go when she is better.

PARENTHESES
1. a. Lucy had a cold (she always gets colds) so we had to stay at home.
   b. I think I might take a nap — hey! I've missed . . .
   c. Here, Mel, take these plates — they're Mum's best ones — to the kitchen.
   d. I — er — thought you might be asleep.
   e. I didn't want to — don't be silly.
   f. She gave me the change (fourteen shillings and sixpence) to put into the cash box.
   g. Try writing a book — a really good book — like *My Cousin, Rachel*.
   h. Put this up on — the light's gone out!
   i. Edwin (the choir leader) has got engaged.
   j. You should see his ring — very expensive!

PART THREE

TRANSITIVE AND INTRANSITIVE
1. *Transitive*
   sang (his . . . tune)
   had (exciting plans)
   bought (some . . . pegs etc)
   had given (some money)
   left (shop)
   pack (his gear)

   Intransitive
   slipped
   hurried (out)
   jumped
   pedalled
   was
   shone
   blew

   was going
   called
   splashed (out)
   double
   was
   smiled
   pedalled

VOICE: ACTIVE AND PASSIVE
1. a. The vase was knocked over by Darcy.
   b. A whole bowl of sugared almonds was eaten by Maggie.
   c. The huge dog was let off its chain by Helmut.
   d. All the string was used by us on the cubbyhouse.
   e. You will be rung by Max in the morning.
   f. He was hit on the head by the falling branch.
   g. The dinner was burnt by Mum when the door was answered (by her).
   h. The trailer was left on jacks (by him) all night.
   i. That tree can be chopped down by you in the morning.
   j. The tarmac was laid and the road rolled (by them).

2. a. They built this thatched house in the nineteenth century.
   b. The thatchers cut lengths of grass into convenient handfuls.
   c. They use the binder knot for the purpose.
   d. They thread long sticks through the bunches.
   e. They wire these onto the rafters or support (them) by wooden pegs.
   f. They prepare each layer on the ground and then lift (it) into place.
   g. The thatched roof kept the house very cool.
   h. They bury interlocking forked sticks in the ground when they build tribal huts.
   i. Bush dwellers keep provisions for long periods in huts with mud floors, which they wet every morning.
   j. Heavy rains damage the huts every year and (they) repair (them) again before the next season.

PERFECT TENSES
1. a. left   b. gone   c. driven   d. paid   e. brought
   f. hurried   g. taken off   h. gasped   i. made

2. a. shall have/gone/been   b. has forgotten   c. has been
   d. has ridden   e. have kept   f. have fallen
   g. have spent   h. have had   i. has broken
   h. have caught

3. a. past   b. present continuous   c. past perfect
   d. future (passive)   e. past continuous   f. present
   g. present perfect   h. future   i. present, future
   j. future perfect   k. present (ie What a lovely house this *is*!)

PARTICIPLES
1. lost (adjective) ridden (verb) thinking (verb) forgotten (verb) turning (noun) fallen (adjective) lying (adjective) broken (adjective) strewn (verb) worried (adjective) excited (adjective) found (verb) climbing (noun) exploring (noun) turning (adjective) followed (verb) setting (adjective) dazzling (verb) bewildered (adjective) fallen (verb) beaten (adjective) lost (adjective) daunting (adjective) experienced (adjective)

Answers to exercises

PART FOUR

CASE
1. a. people (nom), calculators (acc)
   b. mathematician (nom), machine (acc)
   c. machine (nom), calculator (nom)
   d. calculators (nom), operations (acc)
   e. this (nom), calculator (nom), Dad's (gen), battery (acc)
   f. Dale (voc), me (dat), calculator (acc), mine (nom), battery (acc)
   g. memory (nom), place (nom)
   h. You (nom), friends (dat), trick (acc)
   i. I (nom), it (acc), Dale's (gen) book (acc)
   j. Peter (voc), you (nom), me (dat), trick (acc)

PHRASES
4. The stiffening rope (noun), round our hands (adverb), up the tracks (adverb), in the air (adverb), sharp daggers of cold (noun), from the edge of night (adverb), in the dense woods (adverb), on our exposed slope (adjective), with the afternoon glow (adverb), for the last time (adverb), in the twilight (adverb), in our veins (adverb), in a web of ice magic (adverb), behind us (adverb), to a blueness (adverb), from the sky (adverb), over the snow (adverb)

CLAUSES
3. a. If . . . money (conditional)
   b. After . . . over (time)
   c. so that . . . condition (purpose)
   d. as . . . field (time)
   e. as . . . could (comparison)
   f. Although . . . raining (concession)
   g. so that . . . tackle (result)
   h. where . . . muddy (place)
   i. as if . . . it (manner)
   j. because . . . shield (reason)

5. when we recounted . . . speed (adv time mod. 'staggering')
    till . . . woods (adv time mod. 'stayed out')
    the lamplight . . . house (adv time mod. 'stayed out')
    such (that) we felt . . . watching (adv result mod. 'were')
    when . . . wings (adv mod. 'seemed')
    lest . . . pageant (adv purpose mod. 'walked')
    which . . . west (adj qual. 'pageant')
    we were . . . earth (noun obj. of 'thought')
    who saw it. (adj qual. 'people')
    which . . . possession (adj qual. 'sky')

SENTENCE ANALYSIS
1. a. *Finite verbs:* was needed, would slip away, lived.
       Main clause A: Every weekend . . . Robbie would . . . hideaway.
           link: if

	Sub clause 1:	he . . . shop (Adv. cl. of condition, mod. verb 'would slip away', clause A)
	Link:	where
	Sub clause 2:	where . . . lived (Adj. cl. qual. noun 'hideaway', clause A)
b.	Finite verbs:	were, were, shared, sat
	Main clause A:	They . . . mates
	Link:	although
	Sub clause 1:	there . . . them (Adv. cl. of concession mod. verb 'were', clause A)
	Link:	who
	Sub clause 2:	who . . . secret (Adj. cl. qual. noun 'mates', clause A)
	Link:	as
	Sub clause 3:	they . . . evenings (Adv. cl. time mod. verb 'shared', clause 2)
c.	Finite verbs:	come, hung up, might see, was
	Main clause A:	old . . . lantern
	Link:	when
	Sub clause 1:	the heavy . . . valley (Adv. cl. time mod. verb 'hung up', clause A)
	Link:	so that
	Sub clause 2:	any . . . see (Adv. cl. purpose mod. verb 'hung up' clause A)
	Link:	that
	Sub clause 3:	shelter . . . handy (Noun cl. obj. verb 'see', clause 2)
d.	Finite verbs:	was, forgot, had told, had been
	Main clause A:	In later years, he . . . forgot
	Link:	when
	Sub clause 1:	Robbie . . . man (Adv. cl. time mod. verb 'forgot', clause A)
	Link:	what
	Sub clause 2:	old . . . bush (Noun cl. obj. verb 'forgot', clause A)
	Link:	which
	Sub clause 3:	which . . . long (Adj. cl. qual. noun 'bush', clause 2)
c.	Finite verbs:	thought, would like, could live, seemed made
	Main clause A:	He . . . thought
	Link:	that
	Sub clause 1:	he . . . too (Noun cl. obj. verb 'thought', clause A)
	Link:	so that
	Sub clause 2:	he . . . city (Adv. cl. purpose mod. verb 'would like', clause 1)
	Link:	which
	Sub clause 3:	which . . . inhabitants (Adj. cl. qual. noun 'city', clause 2)
	Link:	who
	Sub clause 4:	who . . . it (Adj. cl. qual. noun 'inhabitants', clause 3)

PART FIVE

SOME COMMON MISTAKES EXPLAINED

1.	a.	did	b.	saw	c.	did	d.	have seen	e.	did
2.	a.	me	b.	I	c.	me	d.	me	e.	I
3.	a.	who	b.	whom	c.	who	d.	whom	e.	whom
4.	a.	from	b.	from	c.	from				

Answers to exercises

5. a. That dog does not have (has not got) a tail.
   b. My father has hardly (hasn't got much) hair.
   c. He can hardly kick any goals these days.
   d. I had never (hadn't ever) seen my Grandpa before.
6. a. higher b. oldest c. taller d. more often
   e. better, most
7. a. like b. as though c. as though d. like
   e. as though

KNOW THE DIFFERENCE

1. a. effect b. affect c. effect d. affect e. effect
2. a. illusion b. allusion c. elusion d. illusion e. allusion
3. a. all ready b. already c. already d. all ready
   e. alright f. alright g. all right h. all right
4. a. a number b. an amount c. number d. number e. amount
5. a. anti b. ante c. ante d. anti e. anti
6. a. among b. among c. between d. between e. among
7. a. beside b. besides c. besides d. beside e. beside
8. a. borrow b. lend c. borrow d. borrow e. lend
9. a. burst b. burst c. burst
10. a. censure b. censor c. censor d. censure e. censor
11. a. compliment b. complement c. compliments
    d. complement e. compliment
12. a. include b. include c. comprise
    d. include e. comprise
13. a. continual b. continuous c. continuous
    d. continual e. continual
14. a. council b. counsellor c. counsels
    d. council e. councillors
15. a. uninterested b. disinterested c. disinterested
    d. uninterested e. uninterested
16. a. eligible b. legible c. illegible d. eligible e. eligible
17. a. farther b. farther, farther c. further d. further e. farther
18. a. well b. well c. good, well
    d. good, good e. good, well
19. a. historic b. historical c. historic
    d. historic e. historical
20. a. whether b. if c. whether d. if e. whether
21. a. incredible b. incredulous c. incredible
    d. incredible e. incredulous
22. a. liable b. liabel c. libel d. liable, libel e. libel
    f. liable g. liable
23. a. laid b. laid c. lain
    d. lying, laying e. lay/was lying
24. a. practice b. practise c. practise d. practise e. practise
25. a. principal b. principal c. principle d. principal
    e. principle
26. a. meter b. metres c. meter d. metre e. meter
27. a. stationery b. stationary c. stationery
    d. stationary e. stationary
28. a. them b. those c. those, them d. those
    e. them, those

Index

A
Abbreviations 65-66, 75
Abstract noun 12
Accusative case 111-112
Active voice 91, 94
Adjectives 31-35
    comparison 32-33
    numeral 34
    possessive 33
    from participles 34-35, 98-99
Adjectival clauses 120-121
Adjectival phrases 116
Adverbs 36-37
    modifying adjectives 36
    modifying adverbs 37
    modifying verbs 36
Adverbial clauses 121-127
Adverbial compounds 38-39, 43-44
Adverbial phrases 116-117
Analysis of sentences 130-132
Apostrophe 74-76
Articles 40-41
Auxiliary verbs 25-26, 92

B
Be, verb to be 26
Brackets *see* parentheses

C
Capital letters 63-64
Case 111-115

Clauses 46, 119-129
    adjectival 120-121
    adverbial 121-127
    noun 128-129
    subordinate 48
Collective noun 11
Colon 79
    semi 77-78
Comma 67-68
Common noun 11
Comparison
    adjectives 32-33
    adverbial clause of 125-127
Complement 29-30
Complex sentences 47, 48
Compound/complex sentences, 48-49, 130-132
Compound sentences 47
Concession, adverbial clause of 125
Condition, adverbial clause of 123
Conjunctions 41, 119-120
Continuous tenses 28

D
Dashes 81
Dative case 112
Definite article 41
Degree 32-33
    adverbial clause of 125-127
Demonstrative pronouns 17

Index

Direct and indirect speech 64, 67-68
Direct object 23
Distributive pronouns 18-19

E
Emphatic tenses 96-97
Exclamation mark 70-71

F
Feminine gender 12
Finite verb 20, 45
Full stop 65-66
Future tense 21
Future perfect tenses 93

G
Gender 12
Genitive case 112-113
Gerund 100-101

H
Have, verb to have 26

I
Imperative mood 102
Indefinite adjectives 34
Indefinite article 40
Indefinite pronouns 18
Indicative mood 102
Indirect object 23-24
Infinitive 20
Interjections 41
Interrogative pronouns 17-18
Intransitive verbs 89-90
Inverted commas 72-73
Irregular verbs 27
Its and It's 76

M
Manner, adverbial phrase of 117
Masculine gender 12
May
   in subjunctive 103
   may or can 151
Mood, kinds of 102-103

N
Names and titles 73
Neuter gender 12-13
Nominative case 111
Noun
   kinds of 11-13
   clauses 128-129
   phrases 117-118
Numeral adjectives 34

O
Object
   direct 23
   indirect 23

P
Parentheses 80
Parsing 42-44
   adverbial compounds 43-44
   sentences 42-43
   words 42-43
Participles 24-25, 98-99, 100-101
Parts of speech 11-49
Passive voice 91, 95
Past
   participle 25
   perfect 93
   tenses 21
Perfect tenses 92-95
Person 24
Personal pronouns 14-15
Phrases 46
   kinds of 116-118
Place
   adverbial clause of 122
   adverbial phrase of 117
Pluperfect 93
Plurals 12, 74-75, 76
Possessive
   adjectives 76
   nouns 13
   pronouns 15-16, 76
Predicate 45
Prepositions 38-39
Present
   participle 24-25
   perfect 92
   tense 20

Index

Principal clause 46-48
Pronouns, kinds of 14-19
Proper noun 11
Purpose, adverbial clause of 124

Q
Qualifying
    adjectives 31
    clauses 120-121
    phrases 116
Question mark 69

R
Reason
    adverbial clause of 122-123
    adverbial phrase of 117
Reflexive pronouns 17
Regular verbs 26-27
Relative pronouns 16
Result, adverbial clause of 124-125

S
Semicolon 77-78
Sentences 45-49, 111-132
    kinds of 46-49
    structure 45-46
    parsing 42-43
Simple sentences 46-47
Simple tenses 28
Singular 12, 74
Strong verbs 27
Subject 21-22
Subjunctive mood 103
Subordinate clauses 48, 119-129

T
Time
    adverbial clause of 121-122
    adverbial phrase of 116-117
Tense, kinds of 20-21, 28, 92-95
Transitive verbs 89

V
Verbs 20-30, 89-103
    auxiliary 25-26
    forms *see* tense
Vocative case 113
Voice 91

W
Weak verbs 27